BECOMING FREUD

Becoming Freud

The Making of a
Psychoanalyst

———◆◆◆———

ADAM PHILLIPS

Yale

UNIVERSITY
PRESS

New Haven and London

Yale University Press books may be purchased in quantity for educational,
business, or promotional use. For information, please e-mail
sales.press@yale.edu (U.S. office) or sales@yaleup.co.uk (U.K. office).

Set in Janson type by Integrated Publishing Solutions, Grand Rapids, Michigan.
Printed in the United States of America.

Frontispiece: Sigmund Freud with Martha Bernays, 1883.

The Library of Congress has cataloged the hardcover edition as follows:

Phillips, Adam, 1954–
Becoming Freud : the making of a psychoanalyst / Adam Phillips.
    Pages   cm. — (Jewish lives)
Includes bibliographical references and index.
ISBN 978-0-300-15866-3 (hardback)
1. Freud, Sigmund, 1856–1939. 2. Psychoanalysts—Biography. I. Title.
BF109.F74P485 2014
150.19′52092—dc23
[B]
2013048573

ISBN 978-0-300-21983-8 (pbk.)

A catalogue record for this book is available from the British Library.

10 9 8 7 6 5 4 3 2 1

For Stephen Greenblatt and Ramie Targoff

. . . these psychoanalytical matters are intelligible only if presented in pretty full and complete detail, just as an analysis really gets going only when the patient descends to minute details from the abstractions which are their surrogate. Thus discretion is incompatible with a satisfactory description of an analysis; to provide the latter one would have to be unscrupulous, give away, betray, behave like an artist who buys paints with his wife's house-keeping money or uses the furniture as firewood to warm the studio for his model. Without a trace of that kind of unscrupulousness the job cannot be done.

—Freud to Oscar Pfister, 5 June 1910

CONTENTS

1

Freud's Impossible Life:
An Introduction

What right does my present have to speak of my
past? Has my present some advantage over my past?
—*Roland Barthes by Roland Barthes*

THE STORY OF FREUD'S LIFE is easily told. He was born in
1856 in Freiberg in Moravia, a town now called Pribor in the
Czech Republic, but then part of the Hapsburg Empire. One
hundred and fifty miles north of Vienna, it was a small market
town, almost entirely Catholic but with a tiny Jewish community. Freud's father was a merchant, trading mostly in wool, and
Sigmund Freud was the first of seven children—five daughters
and two sons—of his father's second (and possibly third) marriage to a woman twenty years younger than himself. Jacob
Freud had two sons from a previous marriage. His business col-
lapsed when Freud was three and a half, and the family moved

first to Leipzig in Germany for a year and then on to Vienna, where Freud lived until 1938. Freud went to the Sperl Gymnasium, a school in Vienna in 1865, and after briefly considering a career in law Freud studied medicine at the University of Vienna between 1873 and 1882, specializing in his third year in Comparative Anatomy. After research in physiology but with no obvious professional prospects—he went in 1885 to study for several months in Paris with the great neurologist Charcot, returning in 1886 to set up his own private practice as "Docent in Neuropathology." In the same year, after a four year engagement, he married Martha Bernays, a woman five years younger than himself and the granddaughter of a distinguished German-Jewish family (her grandfather had been the Chief Rabbi of Hamburg). The couple had six children, three daughters and three sons, in fairly quick succession. In 1896 Freud's father died at the age of eighty-one.

Through extensive clinical work, at first using the method of hypnotism on so-called hysterical patients; and through a series of passionate relationships with men—most notably the physician Josef Breuer (b. 1842), whom he met in the late 1870s, and Wilhelm Fliess (b. 1858), an ear, nose, and throat specialist from Berlin whom he met in 1887; and then, after the turn of the century with younger men, most notably Carl Jung (b. 1875), Alfred Adler (b. 1870), Karl Abraham (b. 1877), Otto Rank (b. 1884), and Sandor Ferenczi (b. 1873)—Freud invented the clinical practice of psychoanalysis (he first used the term in 1896). Psychoanalysis was, as one early patient called it, a "talking cure," the doctor and the patient doing nothing but talk together. The patient lay on a couch, with the analyst sitting behind him, and was instructed to "free-associate" i.e., say whatever came into his head, including his dreams, undistracted by the analyst's responses, with the doctor clarifying and interpreting and reconstructing the patient's childhood experiences; but not using drugs or physical contact as part of the treatment. The aim was the modification of symptoms and the alleviation of suffering through redescription.

A prolific writer, from 1886 to his death in 1939, Freud published what in the Standard Edition—the official translation of nearly all his work into English—became twenty-three volumes of theoretical and clinical writing, and he wrote thousands of letters. It was through *Studies On Hysteria* (written with Breuer, 1895), *The Interpretation of Dreams* (1900), *Three Essays on the Theory of Sexuality* (1905), *Jokes and Their Relation to the Unconscious* (1905), *The Psychopathology of Everyday Life* (1905), *The Future of an Illusion* (1927), and *Civilisation and Its Discontents* (1929) that Freud made his name.

As Freud's work became known beyond the confines of Vienna through his writing and his personal influence, the Psychoanalytic Movement, as it was soon called, grew out of the informal Wednesday Evening Meetings started by Freud in 1902 for curious and interested fellow professionals. The first International Psycho-Analytical Congress was held in Salzburg in 1908, and in 1910 the International Psycho-Analytical Association was founded. In 1909 Freud made his first and only trip to America to lecture at Clark University in Worcester, Massachusetts.

In 1917, during the First World War, in which his sons saw active service, Freud discovered a growth on his palate which was finally diagnosed in 1923 as cancer which, despite operations, he suffered from intermittently for the rest of his life, though he continued to work to the very end. In 1919 his favourite daughter Sophie died of influenza at age twenty-six, and in 1930 his mother died at the age of ninety-five. In 1938, after living and working in Vienna for nearly sixty years, Freud fled to London from the Nazis with his daughter Anna, also a psychoanalyst, where he died in 1939.

The facts of a life—and indeed the facts of life—were among the many things that Freud's work has changed our way of thinking about. Freud's work shows us not merely that nothing in our lives is self-evident, that not even the facts of our lives speak for themselves; but that facts themselves look different from a psychoanalytic point of view. "The facts in psychoanalysis," Freud wrote, "have a habit of being rather more complicated than we like. If they were as simple as all that, perhaps, it might not have needed psychoanalysis to bring them to light."[1] Because we want to like our facts we are always tempted to simplify them. Psychoanalysis reveals complications that we would rather not see; before psychoanalysis, Freud suggests, the facts seemed simple, but now they seem complicated. "Bringing to light" might mean recovering something buried, or seeing something in a new light. Freud is not saying here that psychoanalysis has revealed new facts, but that it has revealed new aspects of the facts. The facts were always there, but now we can see them differently. What complicates the facts, in Freud's view, is what he will come to call unconscious desire (so, for example, the fact that Freud invented psychoanalysis mostly out of conversations with men but through the treatment mostly of women—that psychoanalysis was a homosexual artifact—can tell us something about Freud's homosexual and heterosexual desire, what he wanted men and women for; our desires inform our facts and our fact-finding). He will show us how and why we bury the facts of our lives, and how, through the language of psychoanalysis, we can both retrieve these facts and describe them in a different way. Though his writing is dominated, for reasons which will become clear, by archaeological analogies—by the archaeologist as hero—the practice of psychoanalysis was, Freud increasingly discovered, difficult to find analogies for. What Freud was in no doubt about, though, was the value of heroism, and of the discovery of psychoanalysis as somehow a heroic project. His writing is studded with references to great men—Plato, Moses, Hannibal, Michelangelo, Leonardo da Vinci, Goethe, Shakespeare, among others—most of them artists; and all of them, in Freud's account, men who defined their moment, not men struggling to assimilate to their societies, like many of the Jews of Freud's generation; self-defining men, men pursuing their own truths against the constraints of tradition. In the young Freud's myth of his own heroism, created in *The Interpretation of Dreams*, he was a man who would face, in a new way, the facts of his own life (he uses as his epigraph to the book a line—appropriately given his ambitions—from Virgil's *Aeneid*, "If I can't bend those above, I'll stir the lower regions"). Through psychoanalysis the introspective hero born of romanticism went in search of scientific legitimacy. But heroism—not to mention scientific legitimacy—was another cultural ideal that would look different after psychoanalysis. What Freud would realize through his new science—and the devastation of the First World War would confirm this—was that the idea of heroism was an attempted self-cure for our flagrant vulnerability. Freud intimated, through psychoanalysis, that there might be other ways of finding life impressive, other pleasures that might sustain us.

We spend our lives, Freud will tell us in his always lucid prose, not facing the facts, the facts of our history, in all their complication; and above all, the facts of our childhood. Freud sees modern adults as people who cannot recover from their childhoods; as people who have a child's view of what an adult is. He will show us how ingenious we are at not knowing ourselves, and how knowing ourselves—or the ways in which we have been taught to know ourselves, not least through the conventions of biography and autobiography—has become the problem rather than the solution. What we are suffering from, Freud will reveal, are all the ways we have of avoiding our suffering; and our pleasure, Freud will show us—the pleasure we take in our sexuality, the pleasure we take in our violence—is the suffering we are least able to bear. And to face all these improbable facts we need a different way of listening to the stories of our lives, and a different way of telling them. And, indeed, a different story about pleasure and pain; a story about nothing but the psychosomatic development of the growing child in the family, and the individual in his society; and a story with no religion in it. Instead of God as the organizing idea, there was the body in the family; the family that brings its own largely unknowable transgenerational history to the culture it finds itself in. Psychoanalysis, which started as an improvisation in medical treatment, became at once, if not a new language, a new story about these fundamental things, and a new story about stories. For Freud the modern individual is ineluctably, compulsively a biographer and an autobiographer. And his sexuality and his symptoms are among the forms his life story takes.

The body treated only with words inevitably linked Freud, as a doctor, with the more literary arts. Indeed he was slightly bemused to discover that his early case histories—in which, as he wrote, there is "an intimate connection between the story of a patient's sufferings and the symptoms of his illness"—read, as he put it, "like short stories" (or as "novellas," in the new Penguin Freud translation).[2] In a psychoanalytic treatment patients tell the story of their lives by saying whatever comes into their heads. It is an unusual way of telling a story, and of giving and taking a history. So one of the first casualties of psychoanalysis, once the facts of our lives are seen as complicated in the Freudian way, is the traditional biography. After psychoanalysis all our narratives of the past—indeed, all our coherence and plausibility—are suspect. They hide more than they seek. History begins to sound like fiction, and fiction begins to sound peculiarly wishful.

So the history of the period of Freud's time and place—the background, as it were, of traditional biography—can also be read with these new Freudian complications in mind; not that the historical facts are not true, but that the telling of them might be prone to simplification, and particularly when they are at their most devastating. We have to be attentive to the wishfulness at work even in our most painful stories; especially in our most painful stories. Freud lived through, in what is by now a familiar account, the collapse of the Austro-Hungarian Empire and the rise of nationalism; the cataclysm of the First World War and the buildup to the Second World War; the emergence of communism and the rise of fascism; the increasing emancipation of the Jews and the beginnings of their possible extinction. It was an era of fragile democracies and unstable aristocracies, of an inexhaustible capitalism and of economic depression, of the "de-traditionalising" of societies, and of an exorbitant arms race. But Freud's work—as, among other things, a theory of reading—wants to undo our confidence in familiar formulations, especially familiar formulations about the past. Freud wants us to be wary of our temptation to make catchphrases out of history, of our temptation to be too eagerly convinced by our fictions and formulations. We are always, in Freud's view, trying to contain the uncontainable. However horrifying the facts, for Freud history is always more horrifying—and so more elusive—than we can let ourselves know; as though he also had an inkling of just how horrifying it was to become (his sisters that remained in Vienna died in concentration camps). Only the censored past can be lived with, Freud was discovering. From a psychoanalytic point of view modern people were as much the survivors of their history as they were the makers of it. We make histories so as not to perish of the truth.

The psychoanalyst is a historian who shows us that our histories are also the way we conceal the past from ourselves; the way we both acknowledge it and disavow it at the same time (to disavow it is, one way or another, to simplify it; to acknowledge it is to allow complication). After "the great Darwin," as Freud called him, another of Freud's heroes, we are creatures of an appetite to survive and reproduce; and because we are desiring creatures in an uncomfortable world we are, like all animals, endangered by our desiring and therefore self-protective. But unlike other animals, who because they have no language have no cultural history, we also feel endangered by our histories. There is nothing we want to protect ourselves from more, in Freud's view, than our personal and family histories. For many people the past had become a phobic object, concealed in sentimental nostalgia and myths of race and national history. Through psychoanalysis—which was clearly a response to these increasingly insistent contemporary questions—Freud tried to work out the ways in which we are unduly self-protective; the senses in which modern people suffer from their self-protectiveness.

In Freud's view we are defensive creatures simply because we have so much to defend ourselves against; our fears of the external world are second only to our fears of the internal world of memory and desire, and both are warranted (it was Freud that made the ordinary word "defensive" such an important part of common currency). Psychoanalysis, whatever else it is, is a dictionary of modern fears. The acknowledged past, both personal and transgenerational, always threatens to destroy our belief in the future; or, as Freud intimated, modern people were beginning to feel the burdens of their past in new ways (with the rise of historical research and scientific methods of enquiry they knew more about them than ever before). We can't, now, take in the true horror of our histories; and this became for Freud, implicitly, a reflection about his own history as a Jew, as well as a more general account that he was keen to universalise. Freud's fear that psychoanalysis could be misunderstood to be a Jewish Science went some way to acknowledging that the history of the Jews might also be somewhere bound up in it.

We take refuge in plausible stories, Freud tells us in his own partly plausible story called psychoanalysis. We fear the immediacy of experience—the immediacy of instinctual desire and the overwhelming pressures of contemporary reality—and so we represent it to ourselves as symptoms and knowledge, our forlorn and noble forms of mastery. So fearful are we in living our lives now we seek as much intelligibility as we can get; but our wish to make sense of our lives—or our wish to make our lives sound sensible, or at least intelligible—has become an ironic acknowledgement of just how unknowing and wishful we are; a measure not only of our terror, but of our overinvestment in progress as the acquisition of knowledge, and coherence as the sign of knowledge. And the "we" Freud was referring to was possibly, he thought, not the fin de siècle Viennese middle class that he knew, but the entire human race. Freud, in other words, in the way of the great nineteenth century European intellectuals, was also a great generalizer. Freud, in actuality, met a very small group of people in his life, but universalising a point—one of Freud's most interesting papers, for example, he entitled "On the Universal Tendency to Debasement in the Sphere of Love" (1912)—was a way of rhetorically enforcing it. As a young man, by all accounts, Freud, like many young people with intellectual tendencies, was more interested in reading than in sociability; and *Don Quixote* was his favourite book. The psychoanalyst he became was as interested in whether we can experience ourselves as he was in whether we can know ourselves; and above all in how knowledge, especially self-knowledge, can become a refuge from experience. Psychoanalysis was to be, essentially, an elaboration of *Don Quixote*.

But one of the things we will notice in Freud's writing is not the dogmatic narrow-minded knowingness for which he has become famous, but an absorbing and wide-ranging skepticism. And skepticism, he believed, needed to be justified, to be accounted for, just as much as, if not more than, conviction and belief. His *Three Essays on Sexuality*, one of the early ground-breaking books of psychoanalysis, ends with what Freud calls the "unsatisfactory conclusion" that "we know far too little . . . to construct from our fragmentary information a theory adequate to the understanding alike of normal and pathological conditions."[3] Nearly one hundred and fifty pages of extraordinary speculation end with Freud's virtual undoing of the whole project. And with the reminder that what we call sexuality is itself a constructed theory, not simply a natural fact. What Freud discovers is the impossibility of normalizing sexuality, and that the sexual is what we always want to normalize. And this is because, he writes, "sexuality is the weak spot . . . in cultural development."[4] So Freud will be inclined to say, as his detractors always claim, that everything is sexual, without his ever quite knowing what the sexual is. Or indeed what it might mean to know about or understand sexuality. Freud, we might say, was interested in sex because it was one of the forms that personal history takes; one of the ways in which knowledge of the past re-presents itself; one of the areas of the individual's life where the biographer and the autobiographer are struck by something, and falter, never quite knowing what to make of it all.

Freud became preoccupied in his work, in other words, not only with increasing our knowledge of human nature, but with those moments when knowing breaks down, when it doesn't work, when something other than knowledge becomes an object of desire (what interrupts our concentration as readers may be as telling as the book we are reading; Freud is always making the case for interruption). We make a Freudian slip when we thought we knew what we were saying. We dream beyond the bounds of intelligibility. We unwittingly repeat what we hate about ourselves. Freud, that is to say, charts the development of the unknowing and largely unknowable modern individual in a culture obsessed by knowledge; of the distracted and disrupted individual whose continuities and traditions are breaking down around him. Where progress was demanded Freud found regression and the allure of the past; where predictability was wanted he found the disarray of desire and self-destructiveness; where laws of human nature or of history were sought he found only, in the title of one of his finest papers, "Instincts and Their Vicissitudes." Childhood, as he described it, informed everything but predicted nothing. Human development was riddled with paralysing repetitions. Sexuality obsessed us, but what an obsession with sex was an obsession about was unclear. Darwin, in Freud's view, had oversimplified sex by suggesting it was really about reproduction. Because Freud believed that everything was "overdetermined," had multiple causes and reasons, nothing could be about one thing. Indeed the history of science showed that new causes and meanings kept occurring to people. Science was as unpredictable as the phenomena it studied; nor could it prove scientifically that it was of value.

So after Freud, if we are to take him on his own terms, our knowledge of his, or of anyone else's, life—and indeed our wish for knowledge about his life—has to be tempered with a certain irony. Because it was precisely the stories we tell ourselves about our lives, and about other people's lives, that Freud put into question, that Freud taught us to read differently. Freud helped us, if that is the right word, to see our lives as both ineluctably determined and utterly indeterminate; as driven by repetitions but wholly unpredictable; as inspired by unconscious desire and only intermittently intelligible, and then only in retrospect. There was the unfolding of the individual's psychobiological potential—the so-called life cycle with its developmental stages—and there was something less surely plotted, less explicable, called the life story. Freud wanted to bring these two inextricable things together in the science of psychoanalysis, but with a great deal of uncertainty about what was possible.

And partly because Freud was discovering that we obscure ourselves from ourselves in our life stories; that that is their function. So we will often find that the most dogmatic thing about
Freud as a writer is his skepticism. He is always pointing out his
ignorance, without ever needing to boast about it. He is always
showing us what our knowing keeps coming up against; what
our desire to know might be a desire for.

It is sexuality and a death-dealing aggression—the subjects to which Freud's work is always returning—that render us
incoherent, that expose the limits of our language, and of our
self-knowledge. There is what he later calls "the silence" of a
Death Instinct working inside us, and an insatiable sexual hunger, "incapable of obtaining complete satisfaction," that resists
our sense-making.[5] And our histories, at their most fundamental, are stories of need in Freud's account; of sexuality and violence and scarcity; of irresolvable conflict and unavoidable ambivalence. Where we love we always hate, and vice versa. We
are wanting more life for ourselves but we are also wanting, in
one of Freud's memorable phrases, "to die in our own way." We
are full of vitality but, he tells us in *Beyond the Pleasure Principle*
(1920), we crave inertia, insentience. We want to get better but
we love our suffering. What Freud increasingly found most difficult to cure in his patients was their (mostly unconscious) wish
not to be cured. In his search for cures, Freud found just how
incurable we are; that is, he found how much pleasure we can
get from our suffering through the psychic alchemy of what
he would call masochism. Indeed, Freud developed psychoanalysis, in his later years, by describing how it didn't work;
clinically, his failures were often more revealing to him than his
successes. By showing us what psychoanalysis couldn't do he
showed us what it was (and what it was up against). It was part of
Freud's considerable ambition—what is a theory of wishing if not
a theory of exorbitant ambition?—to reveal in no uncertain terms
the limits of psychoanalytic ambition. And to reveal that the

causes and reasons of ambition could be found in the catastrophes of childhood. And that we are children for a very long time.

And yet in what Freud saw as our instinct-driven lives there seemed to be a margin of freedom, a place for rationality and choice. He agreed, implicitly, with Swift, that you can't reason a person out of something they weren't reasoned into, but he did discover that he could sometimes psychoanalyse people out of, or through, their most anguished predicaments. There was an Enlightenment Freud who believed we might be more sensible and law-abiding; that knowledge, and particularly the knowledge generated by the methods of science, could dispel superstition, and free us from the old-fashioned tyrannies. A Freud who went on believing in the giving of reasons and the testing of hypotheses, in the beneficial uses of explanation and understanding, in the value of putting words to things; who believed that the conversation he had invented called psychoanalysis could improve our lives, even if it could only, in another memorable phrase, "transform hysterical misery into ordinary human unhappiness"; who hoped that knowledge and desire may not be at odds with each other. And there was an anti-Enlightenment Freud who, as time went on, found it harder and harder to believe in most of these things, and yet without ever losing his belief in the value, and the values of psychoanalysis. Indeed how Freud kept faith with psychoanalysis as it evolved—that is, how what he calls the unconscious never lost its grip on him—is the central drama of Freud's life. It was this relationship between desiring and knowing, between the unconscious and what he called the ego, between ourselves as creatures of (initially uncultured) appetite and creatures of (cultured) knowledge that fascinated Freud. Psychoanalysis became an enquiry into what, if anything, knowing had to do with desiring; and, indeed, about what telling one's life story had to do with desiring. Freud's initial hope was that life stories were sustainers of appetite. His confidence in this, though, was to diminish.

But it was, as Freud was to remark on several occasions—and it is a remark we must take to heart in any consideration of Freud's life—the pursuit of knowledge that inspired him as a younger man (and indeed as an older man). He felt, he wrote in his *Autobiographical Study* (1925), "no particular partiality for the position—and activity of a physician in those early years, nor, by the way, later. Rather, I was moved by a sort of greed for knowledge."[6] Not religion, not politics, not medicine, not sexuality, not healing and helping, but knowledge. And the pursuit of knowledge would be another casualty of the psychoanalytic enterprise, as Freud began to describe it as simply another form our ingenious and ubiquitous sexuality could take. Psychoanalysis became the language in which Freud could wonder what a greed for knowledge might be a greed for. Curiosity, Freud came to believe, was initially and fundamentally about sex. There was nothing else to be interested in but people's relations with each other, what they did together (everything being a pretext for doing something together). The satisfactions of knowing were derivatives—sublimations, to use his rather obscure term—of the more immediate, the more sensuous pleasures of childhood. Not that the person intent on knowledge was a failed sensualist, but rather a troubled one; in thrall, as we all are, not simply to his desires, but to the conflict around and about his desires. Pleasure was not addictive, anaesthetizing it was.

What (some) modern people couldn't help but notice after Freud, through their symptoms, their dreams, their slips of the tongue and their bungled ambitions—especially modern people who were no longer religious believers—was how unconscious they were, how removed from a clear sense of their own intentions, how determinedly ignorant they were about their pleasure. And, in Freud's language, this meant how conflicted they were about their appetites, and so how fundamentally divided they were against themselves. As if people no longer knew what was in their best interests, or what their interests were; or indeed whether they had best interests. Modern people could live as if they couldn't care less about themselves. They would, for example, risk everything or nothing at all for money or for love, for safety or for excitement. It was confounding, after Darwin, to discover that Man, as he was then called, was the animal that deliberately estranged himself from his own nature, that suffered above all, from his capacity for adaptation. In Freud's account it had become all too human to discard survival and reproduction as the aims of life; all too human to adapt (i.e., to assimilate and conform) at the cost of vitality. From a psychoanalytic point of view even the Darwinian facts seemed too simple. Psychoanalysis was to be a therapy in which modern people could work out for themselves what, if anything, mattered most to them: and despite the strictures of science.

Like all writers, Freud writes out of a specific historical moment; but what he often seems to be writing about is just how difficult it is to know what is specific about any historical moment (what the facts are), or what any individual is going to make of her own times (what the facts are for her). Partly because the past so insistently informs the present—our seeing the present in the terms of the past is what he will call "transference"—but also because our reconstructions of the past are inspired by our desires for, and fears about, the future. And partly because of the individual's idiosyncratic psychic metabolism that Freud was unusually attentive to (in Freud's work the individual is always making something of her history, whether or not she is making her own history). The way we digest and metabolize our experience Freud would call "dream-work" in *Interpreting Dreams* (1900). Freud saw the modern individual as excessively overstimulated (both by his environment and his desires), and struggling all the time to become insulated without becoming too isolated or estranged from herself or other people (symptoms were a way of regulating exchange). In what were soon to be called "mass-societies" it was the individual voice, in all its singularity, that Freud was interested in. His emblem for this was his belief that a person's dream could be understood only through the dreamer's own associations to her dream; she had to be enabled through collaboration to be more self-interpreting, less defined from outside (there couldn't be a Freudian dictionary of dream symbols). For Freud we are desiring creatures, creatures who look forward with certain satisfactions in mind; but each with, or through, a different history. All history, for Freud, is the rewriting of history because the past is something we rewrite to make a future for ourselves. And in this sense our pasts are inherently unstable. As early as 1896 Freud referred in a letter to what he would eventually call "deferred action." "I am working on the assumption," he wrote to Wilhelm Fliess on December 6, "that our psychical mechanism has come into being by a process of stratification: the material present in the form of memory-traces being subjected from time to time to a re-arrangement in accordance with fresh circumstances—to re-transcription." The individual keeps rewriting his history even though his biographer cannot (we may want another biography of someone but we don't want another biography by the same biographer). It is, as Freud both intimates and enacts in his writing—in his return to and reworking of the same preoccupations—the inability to rewrite the past that the individual suffers from. And that makes the biographer such an unreliable witness. A biography, like a symptom, fixes a person in a story about themselves.

Freud draws our attention to this work of re-presenting the personal and cultural past in words; when his patients started giving an account of themselves in psychoanalysis it was this work, of distortion and disguise and censorship—work that all too easily becomes inhibited, but work potentially of great vision and imagination—that Freud found himself hearing. He discovered, through his invention of the psychoanalytic situation, that in the speaking (and writing) of history, memory and desire were inextricable, indeed memory was of desire; that our histories, whatever else they are, are coded stories about what we wanted in the past, and about what was missing in that past; and about what we want in the future, and about what we fear in that future. Words, Freud assumed, are the tools of need and desire; and since there can be no history without language, it is the individual's history of needing and desiring that must be reconstructed, as far as is possible, in psychoanalytic treatment. Psychoanalysis enables patients to recover their desire, by re-presenting their history to a new kind of attentive listener. At a time when it was increasingly up for grabs what people could use—race, religion, nationality, class, talent—to identify themselves with (and as), Freud would want modern people to identify themselves as primarily desiring creatures. But with one essential qualification—to desire for human beings was to remember, to remember their earlier forms of desiring. For Freud our (shared) biological fate was always being culturally fashioned through description and recollection.

Freud wants us to remember that need is where we begin and language is what we acquire. Language, as at once a deferred pleasure and a formative adaptation (and estrangement), was at the center of Freud's work; on virtually every page of Freud's writing, as the French psychoanalyst Jacques Lacan remarks, there is a reference to language. Freud's account of the talking cure, unsurprisingly, has within it theories and assumptions about language and how it works, but not theories informed by the modern science of linguistics, which was not then available to him. The individual's always ongoing acquisition of language—his relationship to the language he inherits and the language he speaks—was one of Freud's primary concerns. When he is describing the unconscious and how it works it often sounds as though he is describing the workings of a language; the treatment of psychoanalysis itself was conducted only in words. And Freud was as much, if not more of, a writer than a doctor. He became a writer who, as he would put it in *Beyond the Pleasure Principle* (1920), wanted to "throw [himself] into a line of thought and to follow it wherever it leads."[7] And he would encourage his patients when speaking, to do something similar. Following a line of thought to wherever it leads—to wherever it leads by association—was to be the psychoanalytic way. Until, that is, the need to restore order kicked in.

So Freud's work, we also need to remember, is of a piece with much of the great modernist literature, all of which was written in his lifetime; a literature in which—we can take the names of Proust, Musil, and Joyce as emblematic—the coherent narratives of and about the past were put into question; and, of course, in all the other arts and the sciences; and in the overlap between them in psychiatry, philosophy, and sociology this was a period of extraordinary energy and invention and improvisation. Indeed psychoanalysis makes sense only as part of the larger cultural conversation in the arts that became known as modernism. Vienna, where Freud lived for virtually his entire life, was the eye of the storm of this modernism; and was the birthplace of the linguistic philosophy that came to dominate the twentieth century. Psychoanalysis, as we shall see, was to be at once Freud's resistance and his assimilation to this newly emerging modern culture in which he found himself growing up. And in getting a sense of Freud's life, a version of it, we will need to notice both where he protests and where he complies; what, in his contemporary culture, he found compelling—the collecting of antiquities, for example, and the smoking of cigars; and what he was indifferent to—he had, for example, little interest in contemporary art, and was dismissive of Surrealism, which owed so much to him; he had no interest whatsoever in opera or music, something of a feat in the Vienna of his time. We will need to notice what Freud used the language of psychoanalysis to talk about (childhood, sexuality, aggression, humour, the unconscious, memory, biography, religion, science), and to mostly avoid talking about (politics, philosophy, economics, class, fashion, mysticism, old age). We will have to see, in other words, which of the cultural conversations of the time Freud wanted to join, and which he avoided; what Freud needed psychoanalysis to liberate himself from, and what kind of imprisonment it liberated him for.

In 1859, three years after Freud was born, Darwin published *On the Origin of Species;* in 1939, the year Freud died, Joyce published *Finnegans Wake.* This is one way of imagining the timeline of Freud's life, the disrupted narratives of time and of the times that he lived through and contributed to so dramatically. Like so many of the people of Freud's generation, the world Freud grew up in was unrecognizable to the world he died in; it could only be remembered—or rather, to use a psychoanalytic term, reconstructed—because so much had been lost (Eric Hobsbawm entitled his history of the twentieth century *The Age of Extremes,* and Niall Ferguson subtitled his history of the century *History's Age of Hatred* because a seismic disturbance was being registered). In the second half of the nineteenth century and the first half of the twentieth century— in Freud's lifetime—Europe was radically transformed. And in ways in which we may only just be beginning to understand, or even to get glimpses of. It was not a world turned upside down, but a world less coherent, less able to be pictured than that. Freud's life, and psychoanalysis itself, are glimpses of those times, at once a product of those times, and Freud's protest against them through the choices he made. The new stories and new ways of telling stories—even the ways of not telling stories, or of finding alternatives to narrative coherence, or the philosophical investigations into language that Wittgenstein pursued—were, like psychoanalysis, signs of the times; both symptomatic and diagnostic. They were part of the process of people making sense of, and coping with, their (modern) lives; ways of working out both what kind of sense was now possible, and whether it was sense that now needed to be made. And psychoanalysis—the project of Freud's life—needs to be seen as part of the history of storytelling, as much as of the history of medicine. Certain symptoms, Freud realized, were stories in abeyance, stories waiting to be told but felt to be untellable. There were symptoms where there couldn't be words; where words were forbidden, or unavailable. Talking about symptoms, Freud began to find, was one of the ways in which people could make sense, could talk about what mattered most to them, about what made their lives worth living (or not). Freud read pathology as though it were an uncompleted conversation, a modern way of talking, a language. Psychoanalysis became a story about why people couldn't speak, and about what it was they could not speak about. And Freud himself could speak by speaking (and writing) about these things.

Genius, Sartre once wrote, is the word we use for people who get themselves out of impossible situations. Whether or not Freud was a genius—and genius was one of the many words Freud changed our sense of—psychoanalysis was the conversation Freud invented to get himself and other people through the impossible situations of their lives, the impossible situations that their lives had become in a modern world. A world in which people had to adapt to things—to economic and political conditions—*that may be impossible to adapt to*. And this involved, as I say, giving a different kind of account of what a life story, or indeed of what a history was; both what a person might be doing, wittingly and unwittingly, in telling something of her life—or, indeed, in telling something of someone else's life, which a life story always involves; and what a person might be wanting not to do in the telling of her life. There were things in a life that seemed to resist articulation, and there were things it was forbidden to say.

So a biography of the young Freud—a biography after Freud, in other words—has to begin, has to briefly set the scene, so to speak, with Freud's own misgivings about biography, and about biography as an impossibility. With, in short, the idea of the impossible life. The idea that is at the heart of psychoanalysis; that there is something impossible about the living and the telling of our modern lives. Impossible in the sense that we cannot see possibilities—for leading good lives, for political justice, for living without religious consolation, for sexual satisfaction and relations between the sexes—or that there are none. That childhood is inherently catastrophic, and unrecoverable from; that the mismatch now between childhood and adulthood, men and women, the young and the old, has become intractable (Freud would always be interested in things that didn't work). When he famously said that psychoanalysis was the impossible profession—"In truth," Freud wrote to Binswanger, "there is nothing for which man's disposition befits him less than occupying himself with psychoanalysis"—he was giving us an important clue about the life he had invented for himself.[8] A life, it turns out, that the young Sigmund Freud wanted no one to know about.

Psychoanalysis would one day be Freud's proof that biography is the worst kind of fiction; that biography is what we suffer from; that we need to cure ourselves of the wish for biography, and our belief in it. We should not be substituting the truths of our desire with trumped-up life stories, stories that we publicize. It is, in other words, about biography that the young (and the old) Freud protests too much. As though biography was, as Karl Krauss the Viennese satirist famously remarked of psychoanalysis, the symptom that was purporting to be the cure. When psychoanalysis works, Freud will suggest, it cures people of their need to be their own biographers. But biography, of course, unlike psychoanalysis—though Freud seems to be forgetting this—may be aiming at truth but it is not trying to cure anybody of anything. So Freud's fussing about biography is also his way of thinking about what kinds of truth about a life are available, and what those truths are for. And whether the truth, if it exists, is curative. Why, Freud seems to be wondering when he writes about biography, do we want what we call truths about ourselves, a question he cannot ask directly about psychoanalysis itself? So it is, as they say, of interest that for Freud at the very beginning of his professional life, biographers were the enemy. We need to note that before the invention of psychoanalysis, Freud believed that a life, his life, was not the kind of thing that could, or should, be known about. Or, at least, that life stories were not for public consumption. That life stories were an attempt to mislead. That only certain kinds of intimacy made truthfulness possible. Psychoanalysis became a way of working out what the preconditions were for truthfulness between people. And what that truthfulness could do for them.

Freud, in fact, had a lifelong aversion to biography and to biographers. He was not averse to biographical speculation himself—in his writing there are speculative biographical accounts of Shakespeare, Michelangelo, and Leonardo da Vinci, among others—but his misgivings about biography were a way of saying something important about psychoanalysis. Of defining psychoanalysis by saying what it is not. Or what he hopes it is not. When the writer Arnold Zweig offered to write Freud's biography in 1936, Freud replied with excessive—that is, unusually self-revealing—rancor. "To be a biographer," he wrote to Zweig,

> you must tie yourself up in lies, concealments, hypocrisies, false colourings, and even in hiding a lack of understanding, for biographical truth is not to be had, and if it were to be had we could not use it . . . truth is not feasible, mankind doesn't deserve it, and anyway isn't our Prince Hamlet right when he says that if we all had our deserts, which of us would "scape whipping"?[9]

To have a sense of what someone was like after reading their biography is to have been willingly duped. The biographer deceives himself and others, his subject is exposed as culpable, and the reader is not worthy of biographical truths even if they could be told, which they can't. In biography the truth is neither available, useful, nor feasible. But in psychoanalysis, Freud intimates, which deals with similar material, it may be; the analyst doesn't have to give a misleading account of the patient because he can check it against the patient's account; and he doesn't have to position himself as judge, or indeed as in any way punitive. The private thoughts that are episodes in peoples' lives can never be episodes in their biographies; psychoanalysis would encourage the voicing of private thoughts. Unlike a biography, and indeed unlike Hamlet, psychoanalysis is a conversation, and not a piece of writing (it doesn't have a known beginning, middle, and end). The patient has the opportunity to speak for himself, to answer back, to go on with the conversation; a different way of being truthful is available to both the analyst and the patient. The unconscious has no biography. Biographical truth is not to be had, but personal truth may be; and it may be useful, feasible, and something to which we may be entitled.

And then, of course, there is the possibility that Freud is being so defensive here because he also feels that the analyst and the biographer may be more similar than he would wish—psychoanalysis does, after all, trade in biographical truth—and that something immoral, something suspect about the analyst, is exposed by the art of biography. That the analyst, like the biographer, can never be beyond suspicion (the analyst is no more immune than anyone else from psychoanalytic interpretation; everyone is equally, that is, immeasurably, unconscious). Perhaps the role of psychoanalyst, as many of its critics would say, ties the analyst up in lies, concealments, hypocrisies, false colorings, and even in hiding a lack of understanding; and perhaps what psychoanalysis can only ever reveal is how disreputable the patient always really is. At its most minimal Freud reveals here what the lifelong practice of psychoanalysis had left him feeling about so-called human nature (and we may wonder what the effect of this was on the way he, and his followers, practiced psychoanalysis). Did a life of psychoanalysis leave him feeling like the biographer he described? And were the motives of the psychoanalyst comparable to the biographers who, Freud claimed in his essay on Leonardo da Vinci, "sacrifice truth to an illusion, and for the sake of their infantile phantasies abandon the opportunity of penetrating the most fascinating secrets of human nature"?[10] It was the more intimate and strange conversations of psychoanalysis that was the real opportunity for such "penetrating" enquiries, Freud believed; and yet he couldn't help but wonder how the psychoanalyst's infantile fantasies—the psychoanalyst's buried past—affected the treatment. Nor, indeed, what it was that the analyst wanted from the patient (other, that is, than his money). One way or another Freud—and the new professional he had invented, the psychoanalyst—was shadowed by the biographer. By Freud's misgivings about what the biographer might be up to. All Freud's work as a psychoanalyst was to be about what the experience of knowing someone—including oneself—was like. Describing why and how biography was misleading clearly helped Freud define what he took to be the new truthfulness of psychoanalysis.

At a time when the boundaries between the public and the private life were shifting, Freud, as it turns out, was to become the great defender of the privacy of the self. Psychoanalysis, unlike biography—and unlike the gossip and the journalism that was rife in Viennese society—was also a refuge from the public exposure of everyday life; a setting in which the self—or whatever a modern person was deemed to be—could be talked of and considered in confidence. If the public project was all too often about dismantling (and simplifying) the aura of the powerful—and Freud, of course, was himself to be the victim of this—the project of psychoanalysis was the provision of secluded time and space to discuss the individual's failing powers. And to discover, by the same token, what curiosity about another person—and the other person that was oneself—was good for.

So we must begin the biography of the young Freud with one scene in mind, a scene he described in a letter of 1885 to his fiancée, Martha Bernays. "One intention, as a matter of fact, I have almost finished carrying out," he writes,

an intention which a number of as yet unborn and unfortunate people will one day resent. Since you won't guess what kind of people I am referring to, I will tell you at once: they are my biographers. I have destroyed all my notes of the past fourteen years, as well as letters, scientific excerpts and the manuscripts of my papers. As for letters only those from the family have been spared. Yours, my darling, were never in danger. In doing so all old friendships and relationships presented themselves once again and then silently received the coup de grace (my imagination is still living in Russian history); all my thoughts and feelings about the world in general and about myself in particular have been found unworthy of further existence. They will now have to be thought all over again. . . . But that stuff settles round me like sand-drifts round the Sphinx; soon nothing but my nostrils would have been visible above the paper; I couldn't have matured or died without worrying about who would get hold of those old papers. Everything, moreover, that lies beyond the great turning point in my life, beyond our love and my choice of profession, died long ago and must not be deprived of a worthy funeral. As for the biographers, let them worry, we have no desire to make it too easy for them. Each one of them will be right in his opinion of "The Development of the Hero," and I am already looking forward to seeing them go astray.[11]

At nearly thirty, with no distinctive professional achievements, Freud thinks of himself as a hero, a man who will be worthy not of one biography but of many. And it is essential to the identity of this hero that he has to make a clean break with the past (it is not, we should note, family letters that are destroyed). And this attempt to eradicate not the past, but evidence of the past—not to mention this sense of being buried, of being suffocated by the past—will be what he discovers in his future psychoanalytic patients (one of the shibboleths of psychoanalysis is that there is no such thing as a fresh start). There is the overriding commitment to love and work—the defining values of the psychoanalytic ethos—and there is the reference to the Sphinx, alluding to the myth of Oedipus that will be at the center of Freud's work. But the people he wants to outwit (and provoke), the "unfortunate people," are the biographers; all of whom will have their versions, but all of whom will get it wrong. Freud wants to fascinate and sabotage his biographers. As we shall see, he was to devote his life to the undoing of the biographer's work.

Freud, as a young man, needed to tell his fiancée that he didn't want to be used to gratify the desires of his biographers, their will to know him, to explain him, to sum him up. He doesn't want to be entrapped by suppositions and conjectures and assumptions. Unlike his future psychoanalytic patients he will not be able to contest their accounts. He will go on to invent a version of truth-telling in which no one has to submit to other people's descriptions, in which all descriptions are taken to be provisional and circumstantial; and in which no one is entitled to speak on someone else's behalf (as the biographer can't help but do). The psychoanalysis he will invent will be about how and why people jump to conclusions about each other, and about themselves. As we shall see, Freud had to become his own biographer—albeit a slightly new version of a biographer, but no less informed by prior conventions of the genre—to discover psychoanalysis (if Freud's question was always, what is biography a way of discovering?, his own personal answer would be, the desire of the biographer). After Freud, in other words, we have to ask, what does the biographer want his subject for? What does he want from him? What does he need him to be and not to be? What does he use his subject as a way of talking about, and what does he use his subject to avoid talking about? This makes, in the psychoanalytic way, the omissions and speculations in a biography as telling as the inclusions and the facts. And it makes a biography a double life.

There is, for example, very little on record about Freud's mother, a person, we imagine—and he encourages us to imagine—of some importance in his life; she exists in Freud biographies as a tiny catalogue of personal impressions that tend towards cliché and prejudice ("a typical Polish Jewess with all the shortcomings that implies," and so on).[12] And, as Peter Gay remarks, "there is no evidence that Freud's systematic self-scrutiny touched on this weightiest of attachments, or that he ever explored, and tried to exorcise, his mother's power over him."[13] It is a strange word with unfortunate connotations; not the kind of thing that Freud, or any other psychoanalyst, would have thought possible, or would have recommended. But Freud's mother, in her intractable invisibility, has been, and will always be, an unexorcisable presence for Freud's biographers. More recent biographers of Freud have speculated about whether Freud had an affair with his wife's sister Minna. But whether he did, and what the consequences might have been if he did, can only be more or less interesting speculation. Freud showed us that people's sexual lives are also always a secret they keep from themselves, and why this is so. When it comes to childhood, parenting, and sexuality, the biographer, in Freud's view, is unavoidably at a loss; and in Freud's view these are the very things that constitute a life.

Freud wants us to bear in mind what the biographer might be wanting in his speculations; what the story is that the biographer wants to tell, and why he might be telling it (and why in this way, now?). From a psychoanalytic point of view what is made of the evidence is always more important (more revealing) than the evidence itself; and what is selected out as evidence, and how it is interpreted—what it is used to do—is a function of unconscious desire. Science, Freud soon realized, was sex by other means; what he would call a sublimation. So after Freud, the subject of biography becomes, among many other things, an object of desire for his biographer, at once an opportunity and a temptation. And psychoanalysis, for Freud, becomes a story about what desiring is like for any given person.

There are, then, the deceptions of biography and the supposed truths of psychoanalysis. And the truths of psychoanalysis, Freud would find, are often revealed by the repetitions in people's lives, in the things that keep happening to them, and the things they keep doing despite themselves, and that therefore insist on being thought about (Freud, for example, would keep reiterating his interest in repetition). Perhaps all a biographer can do—at least from a psychoanalytic point of view—is to keep repeating himself by describing the recurring preoccupations that make a life. And allow, and allow for, a measure of incoherence. Freud, as he begins to invent psychoanalysis, is poised between the traditions and conventions of biography and autobiography, and the revisions of psychoanalysis; which would itself become a tradition with its own conventions and rules, however contested. But the Freud who wanted to baffle his biographers, and indeed discredit biography, was also the Freud who would never be psychoanalysed, except by himself. Freud, that is to say, was someone who desired his own descriptions of himself and his life. It is perhaps not surprising that a Jew of Freud's generation would be interested in the possibilities of uncompromised self-definition, and would invent a science that would reveal its impossibility.

2

Freud from the Beginning

I have lost the thread of my discourse.
It does not matter if we find it.
—Gertrude Stein, *Stanzas in Meditation*

BIOGRAPHERS, FREUD KNEW even as a young man, spoke on other people's behalf—like parents, doctors, rabbis, and politicians. Psychoanalysis was to be a medical treatment which enabled people to speak on their own behalf. This would be Freud's interest: what people could say and do, think and feel, if they could speak, as far as was possible, on their own behalf. People's capacity to speak, Freud was to find, depended on their childhood experience (people grow into their past, Freud realized, more than they grow out of it). And the collaborative treatment of psychoanalysis succeeded, in Freud's view, where the biographer would always, crucially, fail: in the reconstruction of people's childhoods. Constructions of and about the patient's childhood that were the essence of psychoanalysis might be—in the words of Freud's late paper "Constructions In Analysis" (1937)—"sufficient" but "inaccurate"; but at least they could be checked against the patient's own associations and memories, however vague. This "work," Freud wrote, "of construction, or, if it is preferred, of reconstruction [an important distinction] resembles to a great extent an archeologist's excavation of some dwelling place that has been destroyed and buried or of some ancient edifice [another important distinction]."[1] And Freud adds, by way of qualification, that "the delusions of patients appear to me to be the equivalents of the constructions which we build up in the course of analytic treatment—attempts at explanation and cure."[2] Childhood for the adult is like an "ancient edifice," a destroyed home, and our reconstructions of it are akin to delusions: and this is a problem for both the psychoanalyst and his patient. The biographer, with less material, makes up his subject's childhood on the basis, often, of mostly written evidence (Freud's mother becomes other people's impressions of her). From a psychoanalytic point of view the childhoods portrayed in biographies are utterly implausible. Worse than delusions.

And this would be even truer, for obvious reasons—the paucity and virtual absence of first- or secondhand accounts—in the case of poor immigrant middle European Jews of the nineteenth century. Perhaps the most important thing about Freud's family was that they were immigrants in the Vienna that Freud spent most of his life in. Freud's youth, that is to say, from the age of four, was that of an immigrant, a resident alien. And psychoanalysis is first and foremost a psychology of, and for, immigrants (people who can never quite settle); not a Jewish science as Freud feared, but an immigrant science for a world in which, for political and economic reasons, there were to be more and more immigrants. The human subject that Freud will describe in psychoanalysis will be a person with little autonomy, subjected to forces he can for the most part neither control nor understand. A figure traumatized by sociability. A person whose desires don't easily fit into the world as she finds it. Freud's life begins, then, not as a story of uprootings—the Jewish communities of Freud's parents' generation were never secure enough to put down so-called roots—but of migration. And as a story for his biographers, it is at once patchy and highly speculative.

I

So the story of Freud's life could begin, say, in the tumultuous year of 1848, the year of failed revolutions in Europe, but a year in which the Jews in Europe stood to gain a measure of newfound freedom. The Jews of central and eastern Europe in the nineteenth century lived mostly in small communities as minority groups in what were often tolerant but hostile cultures. They tended to be hemmed in by restrictions and prejudices and uncertain futures, but they were not perceived as a threat to the states in which they lived (they did not have imperial ambitions, like many of their host nations). They had access only to the resources of their tightly knit communities, and they lived, like all immigrants with, and under, a great deal of suspicion. The continuity of their lives resided in their family traditions, which were religious in origin, their inherited ways of life in a diaspora that had become their culture. For the Jews of Freud's parents' generation the consolations of locality were always provisional; whatever they could identify with and adapt to in their surrounding culture, they would have to be tentative in preparation for the next unpredictable move. Many of these Jews lived a kind of enforced, forlorn cosmopolitanism; unusual forms of adaptation were required of them. No one, of course, can really know now what it was like for the Freud family in Freud's early years, but we can imagine the pressures they may have been subject to; the emotional and economic and political climate that the young Freud had to make his own. His biographer, like the psychoanalyst, is always having to notice and fill in the gaps in the reported story; a story that is always largely undocumented, and such documents as there are require interpretation. The stories of the poorer Jews in central Europe in the nineteenth century tend to be generic, rather than specific due to the lack and limits of such documentation (Freud's parents and grandparents would not have been interested in their lives in the way their son and grandson taught us to be). For these people success was survival. The basic assumption of their lives was that there was nowhere that they could definitively settle; that their fate was to be always potentially nomadic because they had no political or civic status, living always on sufferance in foreign states. The modern individual Sigmund Freud would eventually describe was a person under continuous threat with little knowledge of what was really happening to him. The ego, Freud would write, was not the master in its own house; the rider, he would write, in another telling analogy, has to guide the horse in the direction the horse wants to go. If mastery of one's life, of one's circumstances, is an unrealistic goal, he would wonder, what else should we be trying to do with our lives?

Orthodox Judaism—the way of living for the Jews of the diaspora—was in decline in the nineteenth century, due to the pressures of modernisation. The haskalah—the Jewish Enlightenment that was a version of the more general European Enlightenment—was eroding the old scholarly-rabbinical tradition in favour of a more rational, sceptical humanism, radically suspicious of dogma and traditional forms of authority and encouraging more politically active forms of assimilation. So the European Jews themselves were in a period of transition. Political boundaries were shifting in Europe as nations emerged from the states and empires of the eighteenth century; the status of the Jews within these new nations was unclear. Whether or not they were a race or a people—a much debated subject at the time—they were resident aliens wherever they lived, with an unfortunate and historically ineradicable relationship with their Christian hosts. They brought their irredeemable history with them and it did not endear them to the societies in which they lived. As both the enemies and the inventors of Christianity the Jews were doubly disadvantaged; outsiders in the Christian states and in the more secular states, they were by definition a dissenting group, coexisting with the Christians' defining, sometimes malign dependence on Judaism. The "modern" liberal politics, that Freud adhered to throughout his life, would legitimate this dissent. Indeed, it gave reasons that justified dissent; it gave pictures of political consensus that involved the conciliation of rival claims, rather than consensus based on the repression of disagreement. Freud would construct a so-called model of the mind in which the repression of conflict, the refusal to acknowledge competing (inner) voices, was deemed to be the problem. What modern people suffered from, in what became Freud's view as a psychoanalyst, were spurious forms of internal consensus; symptoms were states of conviction about the self, isolated from differing points of view. But the Freud who would himself become at once a radical critic of religious belief and sexual mores, was a politically naïve liberal in fin de siècle Vienna; a man who, most strikingly, couldn't take the Nazis seriously until it was almost too late.

The Enlightenment critique of traditional forms of authority, of customs and morals that came so easily to the adult Freud as an unbelieving Jew went along with an Enlightenment confidence in the rationality of politics. But before this education in Enlightenment values that Freud was the first member of his family to secure there had been generations of politically marginalised Jews in his family, people for whom political participation was unthinkable. They were among the many people for whom political rights had not yet been invented. Politics was one of the languages that the Jews of Freud's parents' generation were only just beginning to speak. It would be in Freud's life-time that the extraordinary languages of socialism, of Zionism, of feminism, and of psychoanalysis would first become current. But such was their desperation, however unconscious it may have been, the middle-class Viennese Jews of Freud's genera-tion believed they had finally found a culture in which they had a place—a place and a voice. When the French analyst René Laforgue visited Freud in Vienna in 1937, and suggested he leave, Freud replied, "The Nazis? I'm not afraid of them. Help me rather to combat my true enemy." When Laforgue asked who that was, Freud replied, to Laforgue's evident astonish-ment, "Religion, the Roman Catholic church."[3] It was the old, the traditional enemy Freud feared, which stopped him from seeing the new one.

Our vision, Freud showed us, what we are able to see, is sponsored by our blind spots; what we are determined not to know frees us and forces us to know something else. Politics, as we can see in retrospect, was one of Freud's blind spots. The allure of a taken-for-granted liberalism, however wishful it seems with the wisdom of hindsight—the only wisdom Freud be-lieved in—must have seemed irresistible to the Viennese Jews of Freud's generation. A generation who wanted to free them-selves from what previous generations had been through; from what Esther Benbassa calls a "history of the Jewish people . . . long limited to a religious narrative of persecutions and mar-tyrdom."[4] For generations, she writes, this "story of suffering stood in for History in the proper sense of the term" as a way of preserving "the always fragile unity of the community in di-aspora."[5] Freud's generation of Jews—and psychoanalysis, in retrospect, was clearly part of this project—wanted to make a new kind of history for themselves, at once secular and ratio-nal. A history made by them and not merely for them. A history in which more voices could be heard; a history in which more people participated, and in which people could imagine being new kinds of people. "It is not," Freud wrote in the appropriately entitled *The Resistances to Psychoanalysis* (1925), "perhaps entirely a matter of chance that the first advocate of psychoanalysis was a Jew."

II

In the small Moravian town of Freiberg where Freud was born on May 6, 1856, there were 130 Jews, a similar number of Protestants, while the rest of the population of 4,500 were Catholic. Freud was the first son of his father's second (or possibly third) marriage—Jacob had two sons, Emanuel and Philipp, who were twenty-three and twenty-six, respectively, when Freud was born—to Amalia Nathanson, who was twenty years younger than her husband. They had married in a Reform synagogue, and Jacob Freud had renounced, to all intents and purposes, the religion of his Hasidic forefathers (though Freud wrote that his father "spoke the holy language as well as German or better" (quoted in Gay, p. 600). Nothing, it is worth repeating, is properly known about Freud's mother. Freud's father seems to have been a mostly unsuccessful wool merchant. His failing business forced the family to move first to Leipzig when Freud was three, and then the following year to Vienna. Workers all over Europe were migrating to the cities for work, and the story of the Freud family is not untypical for Jews of Jacob's generation who could no longer sustain themselves in local shtetl communities. Between 1840 and 1880 over 200,000 European Jews migrated from Europe alone, and within Europe itself Jews flooded from the East into the cities of the West in search of work.[6] Like other migrant workers their lives had become untenable.

It became the job of the male children of Jacob's generation— and particularly of the first male child, Freud, being the eldest in Jacob's new family, but not Jacob's eldest son; at once special, and not that special—to establish themselves in what looked like a newly emerging more liberal order in much of central Europe. This meant taking up a profession, preferably medicine or the law, for the security of social prestige gained by making an honourable, a respectable contribution to their adopted culture. Jewish communities across Europe were disintegrating, amid what seemed to be both fluctuating economic conditions and the renewed triumph of Enlightenment ideals of free speech, rationality, toleration, and civic (or even democratic) justice. Despite the fact that, as one contemporary historian has put it, "the mythic resilience of Judaism [held] within it a unique power to call attention to the limits of Enlightenment," it was essentially these Enlightenment values that Freud would be consciously drawn to (he would discover through his psychoanalytic work just how tenacious our unconscious attachments are to the allegiances of the past).[7] Freud was born into an escalating clash and melding of cultures in which his family were keen to take advantage of the new opportunities available by relinquishing the albeit diminishing pieties of their past (his father, Freud wrote in 1930, "allowed me to grow up in complete ignorance of everything that concerned Judaism": "allowing" acknowledges a new kind of freedom, a new permissiveness; though the phrase "complete ignorance" might have given the seventy-four-year-old Freud pause).[8] As an adult Freud was to side with Enlightenment values against the "superstition" of religion, while exposing the irrationality of everything human, including Enlightenment rationality itself.

Freud, that is to say, came of age between two worlds, one perhaps dying and one powerless to be born. The world that was possibly dying and that was very nearly exterminated within five years of Freud's death—was the world of traditional, more-or-less observant European Jewry; the world that was powerless to be born was the world of secular liberal democracy, that would be at war with European fascism, within months of Freud's death.

In his work Freud would describe the past as largely unrecoverable from—and give us a picture of the mind as a tyranny—endemically authoritarian and hierarchical in its judgments; in which feudal and fascist states of mind struggled to be more democratic; in which there was a hatred for conflict and a terror of freedom. But he would also describe an inextinguishable passion for pleasure in the people he treated; indeed it was one of Freud's most remarkable (and useful) discoveries that people got pleasure from their symptoms. That when it came to gratifying herself the modern individual had an exorbitant belief in the value of pleasure. Indeed everything could be made pleasurable—the most relentless misery, the most extravagant self-sacrifice, even, or particularly death itself. Modern people, Freud would discover, were by nature and culture utopians; they lived as if they believed in ever more satisfying futures, however much they were suffering. This, whatever else it was, was a revisionary history of the Jews whose suffering, like everybody else's suffering, would look rather different after the inventions of psychoanalysis.

If Freud was not to be an advocate of the so-called perfectibility of man, he would grow up to be a man believing in the possibilities and pleasures of modern people. They could significantly change themselves and each other; and they could be enabled to be the ingenious hedonists that they were (and a story could be told about this ruthless hedonism called psychoanalysis). And all this had begun, one could say, amid the political turbulence of the middle of the nineteenth century (even though as psychoanalysis, among other modern disciplines, would show, the beginnings of every story have a certain arbitrariness). The lives of minorities in the failing Austro-Hungarian empire do seem to have improved after 1848 (the emperor Franz Joseph granted Austrian Jews full civic rights in 1849). But wherever there were Jews in Europe, throughout Freud's lifetime and beyond it, there was always "the Jewish question," about the status of the Jews, their civil rights, and their true loyalties, that Freud, as we shall see, couldn't help but be preoccupied by (one of Freud's last books, *Moses and Monotheism*, published in 1939, was an attempt to prove that Moses was an Egyptian, that the Jews were like all peoples, a hybrid people which they in fact are). But there was a new ambiguity about the status of the Jews in Europe. While the Jews were beneficiaries of the attempts throughout Europe to establish a new liberal order, they were also endangered by the new nationalisms liberated by the collapse of the old empires. Once again the issue would be, where would they be allowed to belong? With whom would they have to begin identifying? And with whom would they want to identify? It is striking, in retrospect, just how quickly—just how wishfully, perhaps—Freud, and other Jews of his generation, identified with German culture, taking its (gentile) history, and above all its literature, to heart.

Part of the legacy of 1848 was the "national question" of how ethnic minorities should fit into the proposed new liberal order; and the related "social question" of the devastating and widespread poverty created by the new economic order. The majority of the Jews in Europe were desperately poor, and they were the traditionally despised minority of Christian Europe; stateless, but with a distinctive and, from a Christian point of view, unredeemed religious and ethical culture of their own. Having made the great refusal of conversion to Christianity, and having committed the great sin of murdering Christ, as antisemites put it, there had been much, subsequently, that they had had to submit to (the nature of refusal, and the wish to believe were also to be reiterated preoccupations in Freud's work as a psychoanalyst). Indeed if there is one spectre, one abiding fantasy, that haunts all of Freud's work it is the prospect of losing everything; and of what has to be lost for the individual to survive, or what the individual fears he must lose in order to survive. In his ideas about sexual development, castration, mourning, narcissism, and the death-drive it is always a question, in Freud's account, of whether the individual can survive his losses, and at what cost? When psychoanalysis is not a catalogue of modern fears it is a catalogue of modern griefs, pleasure being the only cure. So we have to take seriously in any consideration of Freud's life the fact that the Jews of Freud's parents' generation lived extremely precarious lives. And also—and this would have significant repercussions for Freud's generation—that they became an inevitable focus for what the historian Mike Rapport calls "one of the great dilemmas of the modern liberal state," that was created by the revolutions of 1848 in central Europe:

> Should ethnic or religious minorities be obliged to assimilate fully into the political order, effacing in public life any sense of identity other than that of being a citizen, or should the state rest on pluralism (or multiculturalism), which allows all groups to express their own sense of separateness fully, but within a consensus that is supposed to guarantee mutual respect and the rule of law?[9]

The psychoanalysis that Freud began to invent in the 1880s was to be, among other things, a story about acculturation; about how individuals adapt and fail to adapt to their cultures, and about the costs of such successes and failures, such gains and losses, as were possible. Freud—who described himself as "a godless Jew," i.e., as neither an enemy of the state, nor an observant member of his own religion—was to be particularly interested in what was unassimilable about modern people in the processes of acculturation that begin with the child's earliest development. No one, Freud would discover, can ever be "fully assimilated," can wholly identify with or invest in his culture (even if, as Freud implicitly acknowledged, the idea of the unassimilable was itself a product of the culture). The title of one

of Freud's most famous books, *Civilisation and Its Discontents*—
Freud had originally wanted the English title to be "Man's Dis-
comfort in Civilisation"—would sum up both the gist and the
irony of what would be, partly born of his childhood experience, Freud's ultimately disturbing, anti-progressivist vision;
there was nowhere else to live but civilization—all cultures are
civilized in their own ways, everyone needs other people to
bring them up—and we are always, whatever else we are, dis-
contented.[10] The civilizing process was always oppressive, however enabling it was; it selected out the parts and versions of the
individual that were unacceptable to the state, and left the individual stranded with whatever of himself didn't fit in. This, at
least, was Freud's sense of it from his own experience. And it
was this that psychoanalysis would address. Modern people left
with a surplus of themselves that they could do nothing with.
Freud's words for the individual's alternative to culture, for his
inevitable protest about assimilation, were to be "sexuality"
and "wishing" and psychopathology and the "death-instinct,"
the private utopianisms of everyday life. The individual's cry of
the heart against the necessity of civilisation, of acculturation.
And his word for the ineluctable preconditions for this protest
was "frustration." Frustration, presumably, being the common,
and perhaps binding, transgenerational human experience, and
acutely so for tolerated minority groups. So we must, as I say,
see scarcity and injustice, and the difficulties and draws of
pleasure—unsurprising given his family's history—as among the
organizing ideas in Freud's writing. But it was part of Freud's
originality to talk about these things from the child's point of
view, through a story of what he would call, disturbingly, the
child's sexual development, the development of the growing
child's capacity for bodily exchange. And for Freud the child
was also the figure of the immigrant, the relatively helpless
one who has to live, to find a way of living, in other people's
regimes. It was, of course, as a child in his own family that he

would have first both witnessed and experienced the myriad frustrations—and the rationalizations and justifications and explanations of these frustrations of his Jewish community. A community in which very few people would have had any formal education, and very little language other than religious language in which to voice their discontent: a community Freud referred to in a different context as "our wretched, ignorant, and downtrodden ancestors."[11] Psychoanalysis, among other things, would be a (secular) language in which frustrations, and their possible satisfactions, could be felt and figured out.

So it makes sense that in what would become Freud's story of child development, frustration is where we start from. Freud redescribes the transgenerational frustrations of his community in terms of the new science of child development. If, at first, there is something present for the infant which can be called a mother, then there is something that can be absent, that can absent itself despite the child's need. If someone can satisfy us, they can frustrate us. The source of pleasure is the source of pain. This, as we shall see, is where Freud's work begins. And his story of development can be read—in the way Freud encourages us to read, for hidden analogies and disguised parallels—as Freud's way of also talking about authority and dependence; in political terms about the relationship between the state and the individual (or minority group), in religious terms about the individual's relationship with God; and Freud's picture of the child will also have echoes of the antisemite's picture of the Jew, sensual, voracious, and transgressive, the iconoclast, the saboteur in a world of (adult) law and order. The world of what we can take to be the young Freud's prereflective lived experience, that is to say, is everywhere in his adult writing. The past, he was to show us, always has to be inferred from the present, and from our wishes for the future.

Freud's earliest years seem, then, from the little evidence

we have, to have been radically insecure, and he was to discover a huge ambition in himself. But it was an unusual ambition, an ambition to recover what was significant about childhood, and especially about childhood frustrations, for any given individual including, initially, himself. And to find a way of talking about a transgenerational history that had formed him without his knowledge or his consent. And this ambition required a modern secular education, a language that made possible, over time, his ambition to listen, to talk, and to write; to invent a medical treatment made only of words. Everything that mattered to Freud was in the link between language and childhood. Language was the primary tool for acculturation; childhood began without words. Psychoanalysis would be about whatever was without words in a person's experience: whatever was inarticulate or unarticulated, whatever in the individual couldn't speak or be spoken.

In Freud's writing—and indeed, in any account of Freud's life—we have to get used to the idea of language being what he calls, in what is, at least in its English translation an instructive pun, "overdetermined"; that we always say something more, something other, than we consciously intend, and talking about one thing can be a way of talking about many others. As though language itself was determined to exceed what we use it to say. And we have to remember that the adults in Freud's family would have been opportunistically polyglot, Yiddish being their shared and exclusive language. And we also have to remember that for Freud and for reasons, as he would teach us, that came out of his own childhood experience—all roads lead to childhood; language keeps referring us back; referring us back to that first uneasy rendezvous between our bodies and the language they were compelled to use (the analyst will encourage his patient's words rather in the way parents encourage their children's first words). The first "thing" that was once present to us and is mostly absent to us as adults—that was our earliest everyday life—is our childhood; but it became present to us in a real sense, through language. Out of the turbulent, unrooted history of his earliest years, in a Europe undergoing the cataclysmic changes that would issue in two world wars, and in which the Jews nearly became what was referred to by the Nazis as "an extinct race," Freud was to make a story about adult life out of a story about childhood; a story about development out of a story about assimilation. A story about civilization out of a story about immigration. And, ultimately, a story about the individual's elemental desire for extinction.

Freud was not the first person to put the desiring child first—over a hundred years of what became known in the nineteenth century as romanticism had done that (a tradition of writing that he came to, patchily, as an adolescent); and even the sexuality of the child was discussed among some of Freud's contemporary medical specialists. Freud's originality was in the particular links Freud made between childhood and adulthood—between the remembered childhood and the pleasures of the adult, between the language of the child and the language of the adult; between the natural catastrophes of childhood and the troubles of adulthood. Between childhood as a cumulative trauma for everyone, and adulthood as a continual struggle for everyone. Between the child as misfit and émigré, and the adult as neurotic, a casualty of assimilation. In Freud's story of childhood the child's desire always misfires, the parents are never quite enough. And the past is always too much. This, at least, was what Freud was to make of his own childhood. And childhood, he would also teach us, was always and only reconstructed. Childhood was a story adults make up about themselves. It was to be the story that caught on. And psychoanalysis would catch on as a story about why stories about childhood might matter.

III

Because Freud gave us a new way of taking childhood seriously, we can't help but take Freud's childhood seriously. Though in doing this we need to bear in mind, as I say, the paucity of information (in Peter Gay's biography of Freud the first eighteen years of Freud's life take up twenty-six pages in a biography of six hundred and fifty-one pages; Louis Breger's biography gives thirty-one pages out of three hundred and sixty-four pages to Freud's early life). And the fact that childhood is always a problem for the biographer. Like the psychoanalyst he has to decide what is of significance, and why, out of what is always the least documented period of a life. And psychoanalysis, which said so much about the far-reaching importance of childhood experience, makes the biographer's task—as Freud wished—more not less difficult. For reasons Freud was to explain to us, the childhood in any biography—however contemporary the subject—is a dubious fiction. Partly because it is reconstructed from the putative knowledge of the completed life; and partly because children are rarely brought up to be the subjects of biographies. Children live their lives forward, and biographers understand children's lives backward. So with the inevitably scant evidence of Freud's childhood the biographer is reminded of how selective he is being—how reduced the biographical account is compared with the lived experience —and how he is trying to make out a story, finding a plot in something that was never quite plotted. In the telling of this story—which is the making of it—Freud offers us two significant caveats. Firstly, in a paper of 1899, "Screen Memories," Freud shows us that memories of childhood are, like dreams, disguised representations of the desires of childhood rather than accurate, documentary recollections. "It is perhaps altogether questionable," he writes, whether we have any conscious memories from childhood: perhaps we have only memories of childhood. These show us the first years of our life not as they were, but as they appeared to us at later periods, when the memories were aroused. At these times of arousal these memories of childhood did not emerge, as one is accustomed to saying, but were formed, and a number of motives that were far removed from the aim of historical fidelity had a hand in influencing both the formation and the selection of memories.[12]

There are, in effect, no memories of childhood; remembering is purposive but not accurate. What is significant about childhood memories is when they are aroused, and what they have been made for; and, indeed, why these particular memories are selected from so many, to be thought about, and at this moment. And in order to answer these questions at all, Freud proposes, we would need a conversation with the person whose memories they were. And not just any conversation, but a psychoanalytic conversation in which the so-called patient would freely associate to the childhood memory as he would to a dream. Freud once again slams the door on the biographer, indeed upon anyone's speculations about the meaning of all childhood memories, including one's own.

The only thing that approaches truth-telling is done in Freud's invented couple, the psychoanalyst and her patient. Thus Freud creates the conditions in which psychoanalysis is always already a special case; uniquely placed for the understanding of childhood (and of biography, and of the shape and shaping of a life). Childhood memories are evidence, but not of childhood, only of desire (and of desire as fiction); and to reveal the nature of this desire psychoanalytic interpretation is required. Freud, that is to say, believed that he had discovered the truth about childhood memories. But we should note, also, that with the example of screen memories he is showing us not only that any so-called truth is the result of interpretation but it is that which needs to be interpreted. It is exactly what we have taken to be the truth that invites interpretation. Psycho-analysis always implicitly encourages us to interpret its own truths, to read them, to redescribe them; to understand them as screen memories. And in making the least accessible period of our lives the most significant period of our lives, Freud was also implicitly making the case for tact and tentativeness in the understanding of personal history. Clearly, it would be better to talk about the psychoanalytic understanding of childhood as one account among many, which it is; and to wonder, by the same token, why Freud sometimes had such an investment in psychoanalysis as a privileged form of knowledge, while at the same time offering us the tools to resist intimidation and sub-mission? The immigrant, it is perhaps worth adding, always, understandably, has a special relationship to privilege, always anticipates being discredited (like the child, the immigrant spends much of his life being interpreted by adults who know best). So perhaps we should not be surprised that Freud could be so dog-matic in protecting the status of psychoanalysis; and, indeed, the always uncertain significance of childhood.

At its most minimal Freud tells us that childhood memories need to be interpreted; they never speak for themselves. They are revealed in conversation. And that they encode our most fundamental desires. The biographer might be thought of as doing another kind of truth-telling—a truth-telling in the ab-sence of the subject. The biographer can only select the child-hood memories already selected for him by his subject. And out of the welter of experience in the early years of his life three particular memories stood out for Freud, all from his early years in Vienna, and all, perhaps unsurprisingly, about loss, and notably about loss of specialness (it's often the case, as Freud intimated, that the good memories of childhood are taken for granted while the painful memories are registered to be thought over). But we must read Freud's childhood with his own misgivings in mind.

Freud, though by common consensus the favourite child in the family—his sister Anna remarked, "No matter how crowded our quarters, Sigmund always had a room to himself"—had to share his parents with a quick succession of siblings (he was brought up to have a room of his own in other people's minds).[13] Rivalry and ambition, as many people were to remark, seemed to be second nature to him; and rivalry and ambition, as Freud himself would tell us, are inextricably bound up with loss and abjection, at once a redress and a revenge. "Sigmund's word and wish," Anna remembered after her brother's death, "were respected by everyone in the family": "The household became familiar with the fact that Sigi constantly won prizes for excellent school work."[14] In his *New Introductory Lectures*, published in 1933, when Freud was seventy-seven, he was implicitly writing of his own childhood, as though it was yesterday. "What the child grudges the unwanted intruder and rival," he writes about the birth of a sibling with unguarded intensity, "is not only the suckling but all other signs of maternal care. It feels that it has been dethroned, despoiled, prejudiced in its rights; it casts a jealous hatred upon the new baby and develops a grievance against the faithless mother."[15] Psychoanalysis was to be Freud's account of what people could make of the fact that they were not the chosen ones; neither the Chosen people, nor always, or only (or perhaps ever) the family favourite. Indeed the idea of being chosen, of being unduly special, could be a veiled acknowledgement of the insignificant contingency of one's life. Freud was always interested in how the modern individual always and never becomes one among many. And makes a future out of his privation as unique.

Before the Freud family arrived in Vienna in 1860—and moved (twice) within the traditional Jewish district of Leopoldstadt, once the Jewish ghetto, where Freud grew up—his mother had lost a son, Julius, born a year after Freud. And so, we can surmise, Freud would have, at least temporarily, lost his mother to her misery—and then lost her again when she gave birth to a daughter Anna, the year after Julius's death (Freud would call his devoted daughter Anna his least favourite). Freud was born, that is to say, between his father's two much older sons, and the death of a younger brother; between a lost battle for priority and a too violent triumph over a new male rival. Amalia Freud had a child every year for the first four years of their life in Vienna—Rosa, born in 1860, Marie in 1861, Adolfine in 1862, Pauline in 1863—her last child, Alexander, being born in 1866. Freud's mother, in other words, was nursing (or grieving) very young children for the first ten years of Freud's life. He was, that is to say, the continuously "dethroned" favourite. His self-cure for loss was knowledge. And the most striking of his recorded memories from childhood reflect, and reflect on, this.

The first of what I take to be Freud's three most significant childhood memories concerns his devoutly Catholic nursemaid—Freud, we should remember, always thought of the Catholic church as "the enemy"—who looked after him for the first two and a half years of his life; and who, Freud's mother told him, took him to church and, "when you got home you would preach and tell us what God Almighty does."[16] When his mother was about to give birth to Anna, Freud's half-brother Philipp had the nursemaid arrested for theft. Freud was inconsolable and couldn't be comforted until his mother returned. It was only during his self-analysis in 1897 that he discovered—via a series of word associations—that he had assumed his mother had gone to prison. Her absence had, after all, stolen something from him. You want to imprison the person you can love and lose. It was this after-knowledge, nearly forty years later, that resolved this essential perplexity of his childhood.

The second, later memory, is of Freud, around the age of seven, urinating in his parents' bedroom, and his father responding by saying, uncharacteristically, and rather oddly, "That boy will never amount to anything." "This must have been a terrible affront to my ambition," Freud wrote much later, "for allusions to this scene occur again and again in my dreams, and are constantly coupled with enumerations of my accomplishments and successes, as if I wanted to say: 'You see, I have amounted to something after all.'"[17] If you want to find out what is in your parents' mind, or at least what they can say, you have to do something provocative. How, Freud as a good boy might have wondered, will they respond to a rather more incontinent self? What will they or I myself do with, or about, my transgressions?

The third memory, which, perhaps significantly, is the childhood memory that has always been paramount in Freudian folklore, Freud recorded in *The Interpretation of Dreams*. It refers to a story his father told him when they were out walking, and Freud was, as he says, "between ten or twelve years old":

> He told me a story to show me how much better things were now than they had been in his days. "When I was a young man," he said, "I went for a walk one Saturday in the streets of your birthplace; I was well dressed and had a new fur cap on my head. A Christian came up to me and with a single blow knocked off my cap into the mud and shouted: "Jew! Get off the pavement." "And what did you do?" I asked. "I went into the roadway and picked up my cap," was his quiet reply. This struck me as unheroic conduct on the part of the big strong man who was holding the little boy by the hand. I contrasted this situation with another which fitted my feelings better: the scene in which Hannibal's father Hamilcar Barca, made his boy swear before the household altar to take vengeance on the Romans. Ever since that time Hannibal had a place in my fantasies.[18]

These memories seem to tell a particular story. In each of these memories something or someone disappears, and something appears in its place; the nursemaid disappears (as does his original mother), and an insight many years later appears about Freud's fears and wishes about his mother; Freud's well-behaved self disappears for a moment and a transgressive (and ambitious) self appears along with a punishing father; Freud's idealized big strong father disappears, and a weaker, quieter man turns up, along with Hannibal as a new hero. Where there is a loss, Freud discovers, there can be knowledge. Where there is disillusionment, and betrayal, there can be curiosity and idealization; where there is an accumulation of terrible loss there can be imaginative replacement ("It is typically Jewish," Freud wrote to his son Ernst in 1938, "not to renounce anything and to replace what has been lost.") In each of these memories a future is having to be made, by the young Freud, out of a catastrophe. In these memories—if we make them into a story— we can see Freud's abiding preoccupations. The catastrophes would take many forms and would be given many names in the psychoanalysis he would invent—birth, sexuality, castration, the Oedipus complex, displacement, narcissism, mourning, the death-drive. And character would become the transformation, the self-cures, for the ineluctable traumas of growing up. And growing up would be construed as a cumulative trauma of loss; as though Freud imagined that the unconscious assumption of the growing child is that he in some sense owned—his mother, his specialness, his gendered body with all its potential for pleasure—and could therefore feel himself to be continually (or potentially) losing these things. Freud's sensibility, in other words, was elegiac rather than celebratory, possessive rather than openhanded. The legacy of this was to make the profession he invented unnecessarily grim and earnest, keen to promote the idea that mourning is the realest thing we ever do; and that our boundaries are the best thing about us. And yet, of course, Freud would also always be making the case for pleasure; an ironic case for pleasure in which pleasure is so absolutely alluring that it is continually resisted. And in which self-praise is suspect.

The future—Freud being well aware of the prophetic tradition in Judaism—was all to do with the unpredictable consequences of these childhood traumas and their attempted resolutions (just as the profession of psychoanalysis has been so much to do with the traumas of Freud's childhood). Predicting the future, which was integral to the scientific enterprise, was less compatible with the scientific enterprise of studying human nature; this is what psychoanalysis made increasingly clear to him. Prediction was itself a form of consolation, and Freud had too profound a sense of what we wanted consolation for, to be able to believe in it. "I have not the courage," Freud wrote at the end of *Civilisation and Its Discontents*, "to rise up before my fellow-men as a prophet, and I bow to their reproach that I can offer them no consolation: for at bottom that is what they are all demanding—the wildest revolutionaries no less passionately than the most virtuous believers."[19] Freud, and the psychoanalysis he invented, had nothing to say about the predictable future; only the past could be predicted through reconstruction, through the telling of stories about it (Freud "describes past time fondly and in detail," in Malcom Bowie's salutary words, but "his account of future time is foreshortened and schematic").[20] What Freud was intent on discovering—and the use he makes of his childhood memories suggests this—was what kind of future, if any, was recoverable from the past. And what kind of resource the past was in the making of an always unknowable future; the future, as Malcolm Bowie intimates, that is available only in the form of wishes, and the so-called laws of nature. Freud wanted to believe that what you have lost you can recoup as knowledge. This, at least, was what the Enlightenment Freud wanted to believe. The anti-Enlightenment Freud—a darker and more troubled figure—kept coming up against not only modern people's resistance to knowledge about themselves, but also how much through their wish to know, modern people—seemingly persecuted by the desires that were supposed to sustain them—were making strange, confining pictures of themselves. Knowledge seemed a poor container for our sexuality and our violence. And the insistent and often debilitating repetitions in modern people's lives seemed to belie their expressed belief in progress.

The Freud that emerges, all too speculatively, from under his rather ordinary Jewish childhood—a childhood of the times one might say, mostly described from minimal records in inevitably rather novelettish terms by his previous biographers: the failing father, the devoted mother, an uncle apparently imprisoned for fraud, the overcrowding children, the poor warm family in the ghetto—into the new world of liberal education in Vienna in the 1870s had, unbeknownst to himself, two abiding and related questions that would organize his life's work; one more covert, more furtive than the other. His secret question was, what have the Jews lost, and so, by implication, what might they become? And his explicit, his more professional question was, what did modern people have to give up in order to live their lives, and what was the cost of this renunciation?

IV

As a young boy Freud was a great reader. "Not only did he read a great deal himself," his sister Anna recalled, "but he exercised definite control over my reading. If I had a book that seemed to him improper, he would say, 'Anna, it is too early to read that book now.'"[21] It is not an attractive picture, too neatly a portrait of the censorious patriarch as a young man, but also because there is a difference between the person who loves reading and the person who needs other people to read only the appropriate books. It is also, of course, a caricature of a certain kind of studious young man, which Freud seems to have been. Shy about sex but extremely knowledgeable. And an early glimpse of the man who would, in conflict with his followers and his rivals, have a very strong sense of which the right books were.

During his years at the Sperl Gymnasium, where he was educated from the age of nine until he attended the University of Vienna in 1873, Freud was an extremely successful student. "I was at the top of my class," he wrote in his *Autobiographical Study*, "for seven years; I enjoyed special privileges, and was required to pass scarcely any examinations."[22] He read widely, but was particularly good at languages, soon more than competent in Greek, Latin, Spanish, Italian, French, English, but not Hebrew (interestingly Freud thought of his Jewishness as somehow outside or beyond language; "I was always an unbeliever, was brought up without religion," he wrote in 1926. "But enough else remained to make the attraction of Judaism and the Jews so irresistible, many dark emotional powers, all the mightier the less they let themselves be grasped in words").[23] Apart from languages—and language, we should remember, was always the medium and the subject matter of psychoanalysis—it was ancient history that absorbed Freud's interest, the civilizations of Egypt, Greece, and Rome. What has been rightly called Freud's "compulsion for antiquity," his being what he would call later "a partisan of superstition and antiquity" that had begun in adolescence, became a lifelong preoccupation; providing, among other things, many of the analogies for his work of psychoanalysis.[24] Freud seems to have begun his life work of learning the languages of the past as a schoolboy. The adolescent passion was to become a vocation. As a psychoanalyst Freud would become interested in which preferred pasts our actual past prompts us to choose for ourselves: and why these chosen pasts might be so compelling.

But Freud goes on in his *Autobiographical Study*, almost as an association, after mentioning his being top of the class and his "special privileges," to stress that medicine had never interested him. "Neither at that time," he writes, "nor indeed in my later life, did I feel any particular predilection for the career of a doctor. I was moved, rather, by a sort of curiosity, which was, however, directed more towards human concerns than towards natural objects."[25] Freud's misgivings about both science and healing—and, indeed, about there being a science of psychological healing—are linked by the sixty-eight-year-old Freud to the passions and ambitions of his youth. And it says something about the scientific ethos of the times—the positivism that was beginning to dominate the sciences of the time, as they turned against the metaphysics of previous generations—that Freud would think of medicine as being about natural objects rather than specifically human concerns.

But the historical past, like anything that is absorbing, can also be a refuge and a source of comfort. The past as a human concern rather than as a natural object made the young Freud feel better. In his *Reflections on Schoolboy Psychology*, written in 1914, Freud returned to his own school days: "I used to find, the present time seemed to sink into obscurity and the years between ten and eighteen would rise from the corners of my memory, with all their guesses and illusions, their painful distortions and heartening successes—my first glimpses of an extinct civilization, which in my case was to bring me as much consolation as anything else in the struggles of life."[26] Freud doesn't tell us what was so consoling about the "extinct civilisations" that were so alive in his mind and in the minds of many other people—Schliemann dug up Priam's treasure at Troy in 1873, the year Freud left the gymnasium—but he makes it very clear that in these years there was much he wanted to escape from.[27] It is also worth noting that it is not the Judeo-Christian past that fascinates Freud. As with his rejection of the Hebrew language, it was a different tradition that Freud was immersing himself in. It would always be Freud's project to find the past behind the past; as though earlier knowledge is the better knowledge, and the contemporary is too present to be real. There are strikingly few references in Freud's writing to contemporary political life, or to the contemporary arts.

Among the guesses and illusions the adolescent Freud must have struggled with were his guesses and illusions about sex. Though Freud had, as he was to have throughout his life, passionate same-sex relationships in adolescence, there is only one significant (at least recorded) relationship with a woman in these years. When Freud was sixteen he went back to Freiberg, the place he was born, and visited family friends. The thirteen-year-old Gisela was the sister of his friend Emil Fluss, and he fell briefly in love with her, only to discover that it was really her mother that he wanted. "It would seem," he wrote to his friend Silberstein in a formulation that would have been germane to the future psychoanalyst, "that I have transferred my esteem for the mother to friendship for the daughter . . . and I am full of admiration for this woman whom none of her children can fully match. Would you believe that this woman from a middle-class background, who once lived in fairly straitened circumstances, has acquired education of which a nineteen-year-old salon bred young thing need not be ashamed? She has read a great deal, including the classics, and what she has not read she is conversant with."[28] Freud clearly identifies with the mother's struggle to be cultured (he desires something of himself in her); indeed what is desirable about her, in Freud's account is what she knows, or at least knows about. Freud's love affair with the mother was doomed, but his love affair with "education," with the "classics," was very much alive ("esteem" and "admiration" are guarded terms). It was mothers (and perhaps sisters) that the young Freud was interested in—this mother and sister that he falls for live in the town where he first lived with his mother and sister—but cultural achievements were, ostensibly, the objects of desire. It was a self-cure through culture—through the kind of culture represented by this mother—that Freud was seeking. What was the connection, Freud would try and work out, between desire for the woman and the desire for culture? Which was the more dependable, the more consistently satisfying?

It is perhaps appropriate that Freud, who was to become so obsessed by transgression, should have briefly flirted with the law before finally deciding on medicine as his chosen profession. "I have determined to become a natural scientist," he wrote to his friend Emil Fluss in May 1873, in a strange jumble of metaphors, "I will examine the millennia-old documents of nature, perhaps personally eavesdrop on its eternal lawsuit, and share my winnings with everyone willing to learn."[29] "Nature's eternal lawsuit" keeps the idea of Freud as a lawyer in play, and also the idea of nature as a lawyer, with a good deal of evidence in her favor: but does nature have an eternal lawsuit against us, or against everything deemed to be supernatural, like God or the gods? Or against us as the believers in these idols? What is nature's accusation, what is the case being made? Freud had mentioned that it was "the doctrines of Darwin, then topical, powerfully attracted me because they promised an extraordinary advancement in our understanding of the world."[30] It is Freud's curiosity, his "greed for knowledge" that seems paramount in his decision to study medicine; not to mention his belief in his success, and his eagerness to share his "winnings" (learning and teaching were often very much more to Freud's taste than helping and healing). Like Darwin Freud wanted to contribute to the late nineteenth century redescription of nature that was going on in the contemporary natural sciences. It was, as he insisted, knowledge that he wanted, but not necessarily clarity; it is a distinction, a qualification that goes to the heart of psychoanalysis, and that we need to bear in mind as Freud struggles through his medical training towards the discoveries of his new science, psychoanalysis. "Clarity is in science always a falsification!" Freud remarked to his follower Isidor Sadger. "Truth is always complicated and not particularly obvious."[31] Freud would come to believe that psychoanalysis usefully complicated people's lives by disclosing just how complicated they were.

V

At the time Freud went to university in Vienna 25 percent of the students were Jews while Jews made up only 9 percent of the city's population. This, of course, was a mixed blessing for Freud. "When, in 1873, I first joined the University," Freud wrote, "I experienced some appreciable disappointments. Above all, I found that I was expected to feel myself inferior and an alien because I was a Jew. I refused absolutely to do the first of these things. I have never been able to see why I should feel ashamed of my descent or, as people were beginning to say, of my race."[32] He did not refuse to do the second of these things, to feel an alien—"I put up, without much regret," he adds, "with my non-acceptance into the community"[33]—but seemed rather to enjoy, as he did throughout his life, the status of being an outsider, of never quite fitting in. Making a virtue of necessity, this was often the position Freud would take up; he needed to see himself and to be seen as noncompliant, unassimilable. He was able to use what others expected of him for his own pleasure. No one needs the law more than an outlaw and Freud like a lot of Viennese Jews of his generation had to be a kind of double agent. He had, in his words, "the clear consciousness of an inner identity" as a Jew, "the familiarity of the same psychological structures," while wholeheartedly identifying with Austro-German culture, a staunch supporter of the emperor and his empire, immersed in the arts and sciences of his parents' adopted country (though not, it should be said again, in the contemporary arts).[34] Indeed to be a Jew of Freud's class and aspiration involved these divided allegiances; the all-too identifiable Jew and the Viennese citizen had to coexist. Jewish modernity, the historian Leora Batnitzky writes, involved "the dissolution of the political agency of the corporate Jewish community and the concurrent shift of political agency to the individual Jew who became a citizen of the modern nation-state."[35] Once outside the so-called corporate Jewish community, with its separate, more inward-looking culture, the Jew was a citizen for whom citizenship was radically unfamiliar. This was the threshold that Freud—who was to radically redescribe the whole notion of agency—was living in in his twenties. Living between two worlds without seeming to be. And one important way of fashioning this relatively new identity was, as we have seen, through higher education. And, for Freud, through the study of what was presumed to be the universal language of science. Freud refusing to be "ashamed of his descent" was, of course, an allusion to Darwin, who had shown that everybody irrespective of race and class shared the same descent; that we are all descended from monkeys and that we need to work out what we have done to ourselves through acculturation to make ourselves ashamed of these origins. The new Darwinian biology opened up for Freud different ideas about origins; before so-called ancient history, before the Bible there were the great apes.

If Freud had chosen to study law, his original choice, there would have been more obvious continuity between the passions of his adolescence and his chosen profession; but Darwin was the link. Freud was interested in the laws of, and the origins of the preconditions for, what was now more frequently called human nature; the early nineteenth century question "Is Man one species?" was gradually being replaced by the question "What kind of species is Man?" The scientific methods and objects of study that Freud would come across at the University of Vienna promised him a knowledge that was not local knowledge, an understanding and a method of enquiry supposedly purged of prejudice and parochialism; in which matters of class, race, and religion—all topical concerns that were beginning in Freud's youth to be formalized as academic subjects of study—could be redescribed by science, and evaluated accordingly. Once the Truth about Nature became the object of desire, it was hoped everything else—the foundations of culture—would fall into place. And not least that privilege would give way to talent, the meritocratic dream of 1848. Evolutionary biology, a rigorous antivitalist, antimetaphysical materialism, was the new knowledge and Freud, for many reasons, wanted to be part of what was in effect the scientific avant-garde. And saw no reason why he shouldn't be. Now there could really be nature without the supernatural. And yet Freud, as a young man, was inevitably caught in the bind, the contradiction described by Jacques Rancière: "All the sciences [were] now known to be founded on simple principles available to all the minds that want to make use of them" but, Rancière writes, the very society that "opens up a career in science to all minds wants a social order where the classes are separated and where individuals conform to the social status that is their destiny."[36] The new freedom of scientific enquiry would also confine Freud in the institutions and the institutional knowledge that he so much desired, and leave him with an often unconscious ambivalence, a lurking suspicion about both science and the acquisition of knowledge that were to be fruitful in his work as a psychoanalyst.

So when, for example, Freud made the by-now familiar but quite impossible suggestion to his colleague Sadger that, "If one approaches a thing without preconceptions, then one will find something" we can, at least in retrospect, see him recruiting the scientific assumption of his time to assert that it was possible to float free of one's class, race, and education, to abjure one's culture, and be a man without prejudice or assumption; while at the same time presenting himself as a fully paid-up member of the new scientific community of his time and place (no one at the time, of course, in Vienna could or would ap-

proach a Jew without preconceptions).[37] And, we should remember, the psychoanalysis that Freud was to invent would be
a scientific attempt to understand the force and provenance of
preconceptions; indeed Freud the psychoanalyst would discover
that everything we think we know is preconceived. Knowledge,
from a psychoanalytic point of view, begins as wishful unconscious desire. Freud, as the psychoanalyst he was to become,
would call preconceptions "unconscious fantasies," and describe them as both moored and rooted in instinct. The innocent eye sees nothing and there are no innocent eyes. As a self-
proclaimed outsider and an aspiring, but thwarted, insider Freud
would be adept at looking at the law, and the laws of nature,
from both positions, from inside and from outside and from
other positions besides; with preconceptions, and with the
fantasy of no preconceptions. Through psychoanalysis Freud
would study the laws of human nature, but he would also find
himself studying the desire for knowledge of the laws of nature;
and how theory becomes dogma if it is inattentive to anomaly
and falsification and, indeed, to the apparently irrelevant; and
why, therefore, dogma is so attractive (as it clearly could be for
Freud). In the work of knowing, no one can ever know before-
hand what might be of significance. The unconscious, Freud
would discover, was the part of ourselves that sabotaged our
theories about ourselves, that made all our hypotheses and con-
victions and priorities provisional. The unconscious is the part
of ourselves that won't let us settle.

It was the laws of nature that the young Freud was interested in, and, as we shall see, there were lawbreakers of a different kind in both his and his fiancée's family. Like all supposedly
solitary geniuses Freud was unusually adept at recognising and
recruiting the people he needed for the directions he wanted
to take. And like all "solitary geniuses" the ideas about the unconscious, about sexuality, about children that Freud would become famous for were very much around in the cultural ethos

of his time, as subsequent historians of the so-called psychoana-lytic movement have discovered (Freud didn't discover infantile sexuality, or the unconscious, or radical self-destructiveness, these ideas were in the air at the time; he revised, and added to, the then newly evolving sense of what these things might mean). Freud, in other words, wrote the books he wrote because of all the other books he had read. What Freud was to call his "splen-did isolation" was a cover story for the inevitable hints and bor-rowings and appropriations that he took and he made in his twenties and thirties, as an engaged and engaging student, and then as a young professional building up a private practice as a doctor for nervous illnesses ("dream-work" was the term Freud would coin for the way in which we compose what we take in from the surrounding world in spite of ourselves, unconsciously, to shape our desire). So formed and informed are we, Freud was to discover, by the cultures we grow up in we need a bar-rage of what he would call "defences" to survive our immer-sion; and these defenses, too, we acquire from the cultures we grow up in. His university education and his early professional work with people suffering from "nervous diseases" was the seedbed of his own originality. And part of his originality was to show us, as Cocteau would later put it, that originality is try-ing to be like everyone else and failing; that originality and as-similation are inextricable.

VI

But there was nothing, of course, to suggest that the nineteen-year-old boy entering the University of Vienna, who would study zoology with the Darwinian Carl Caus, physiol-ogy with the Helmholzian Ernst Brücke, and where he also took courses with the philosopher Franz Brentano in Aristotle—who would, that is to say, have a thoroughly empiricist, modern med-ical education—would do anything special with his life. Only in retrospect, as Freud when he became Freud would show us, do lives have what look like an inevitability. Freud was, though, a person who knew what interested him; and therefore what he needed to avoid.

Indeed there is a quality in the young Freud that is worth noting; a need to keep his distance, a fear of overidentifying with people, of being seduced, of being taken in; the kind of fear that Freud as a psychoanalyst would also see as a wish (and would later see as a version of the incest taboo, the lure and allure of the mother). And here too science was useful for its skepticism about unconditional assent, and in its commitment to the truths born of experiment rather than of faith or revelation (science as a method for resolving the Oedipus complex, as a form of distance regulation). In his university education Freud could allow himself, indeed he seems to have craved, being influenced and informed by impressive older men; but older men, unlike his father, who were chosen by himself; and unlike his father, highly educated. But in his later relationships with colleagues and eventually followers—but not, as far as we know, with his wife—there would be a familiar pattern: at first devotion, affection, admiration, like-mindedness, then gradual disillusionment, estrangement, and alienation; a more ruthless reenactment of the modern leaving home story, of finishing with people on whom one has depended. This was to happen, as we shall see, with Breuer and Fliess (and much later with Adler and Jung, among many others); Freud needing to reassert a version of his independence, his "splendid isolation." Freud sensing a betrayal of himself, or of his "movement" in the revision of his theories; as though too much exchange was compromising; as though he had to repudiate whatever threatened to assimilate him. Rationalized by himself and later by others into a hero-myth, a story of the lonely genius, the solitary pioneer, it seems to have been integral to Freud's character (and, therefore, of course, also informed his theory-making—the ego as the always slightly absurd solitary genius of the individual's psyche); a fear, one could call it, of being undermined, undone by the excesses of intimacy. That other people, particularly the people one is drawn to, might make one veer away from what one takes to be oneself. Psychoanalysis would be about the fears of freer exchange.

In *Group Psychology and the Analysis of the Ego* of 1921 Freud would describe how "each individual has a share in numerous group minds—those of his race, of his class, of his creed, of his nationality, etc. and he can also raise himself above them to the extent of having a scrap of independence and originality"; and that what he calls "the advance from group psychology to individual psychology" was the surest sign of progress in a culture.[38] There is something of the modern fear of the mob in this, but there is also an even darker thread that runs through all Freud's work, a fear that the individual loses his mind in groups; and therefore, by implication, that his mind was his only hope ("I personally have a vast respect for mind, but has Nature?" Freud wrote ruefully to Pfister in 1930). Freud's suspicions about sociability—his paradoxical sense that the very thing that sustained us could ruin us—would permeate psychoanalytic theorizing. Freud's seemingly unconscious assumption that other people were a threat to the specialness of the self, not that the specialness of the self was itself the greater threat would turn out to be one of the (ultimately controversial and divisive) foundations of psychoanalysis. It would not be surprising—it would be the kind of thought that Freud helped us to have—that the man who did so much for our understanding of irrationality was himself frightened of madness. Freud's fear of groups, his resistance to mysticism and the occult, all indicate, perhaps, not that Freud feared for his sanity exactly, but that he knew how precarious his—and everyone else's—sanity was. And that he equated sanity with a refusal to be as-

similated, to be lost in the crowd. His concern that psychoanalysis would be taken to be a Jewish science was a version of
a greater fear, that it would be taken to be a mad science. Which
in a certain sense it is.

It is one of the strange paradoxes of psychoanalytic history
that the clinical treatment that is based on collaboration—and
was itself an "after-education" in the possibilities of collaboration—should have as one of its founding myths the absurd and
implausible story of the isolated genius. Freud may have needed
a fantasy of isolation to sustain a mind of his own. But when,
for example, Freud towards the end of his life took exception
in *Civilisation and Its Discontents* to the concept of an "oceanic
feeling"—"a feeling of an indissoluble bond, of being one with
the external world as a whole"—he was referring to this fear or
wish not to be too connected, not to be too much the same as
others, not to be immersed; not to be subject to, or the subject
of, the surrounding medium of the culture he happened to find
himself in. "I cannot," he tells us, "discover this 'oceanic' feeling in myself."[39] Identity, Freud would come to believe, was all
about differentiating oneself—or one's professional group, in
this case, of psychoanalysts—from others; or about joining with
a view to separation; knowing always that being a Jew ineluctably set limits to the possibilities of community, if not of fellow-
feeling. So, in Freud's years at university he changes, from being
a keen student—somewhat like a child convinced by some of
the grownups—to being more like a rivalrous sibling and an ambitious adolescent son. Someone beginning to sense his powers, and who doesn't want to be thwarted; someone beginning
to have a project and who is, in the best and worst senses, using
others to complete it. Freud's autobiographical writings are all
about his teachers, not about his peers. All about the subjects
that fascinated him, not about women. A bit about the culture
he was discovering, very little about the culture he grew up in,
and knew.

VII

Freud, four years into his medical education, would, as we shall see, soon identify with the so-called female hysterics he would observe Charcot treating in Paris, and that he would himself begin to treat, women whose symptoms were a radical refusal of any kind of oceanic feeling. Women whose relationship with others, and with the doctors employed to help them, was always in question. Women who were trying to make a case for different kinds of pleasure from the ones on offer, and who were being turned into cases by the contemporary, mostly male medical profession. The first psychoanalytic patients were people who, by definition, did not fit in, people speaking the wrong language, a language of bizarre physical symptoms; a language very unlike the language of science, and for which science suggested itself as the great explainer. These people were suffering, in Freud's view, and in the view of his remarkable older colleague and collaborator Josef Breuer, from the ordeals of intimacy. It would be the links and the differences between adaptation, submission, compliance, and collaboration—between relationship and the alternatives to relationship—that would be the abiding preoccupations of Freud's work. Issues that Darwin's evolutionary biology, in its emphasis on the organisms' competitive adaptation to the environment, had provided a new language for.

Freud, throughout his life after university, was, as we shall see, determinedly differentiating himself from other men, and particularly men he had begun by loving; but after a long childhood in Vienna, a long education in what Sartre was to call the antisemite's invention of the Jew, that Freud was increasingly conscious of in his years at university. It was, for example, taken for granted that in many medical specializations—as in many other professions—advancement for Jews was either blocked or made unusually difficult. In psychoanalysis Freud would describe both the difficulties the individual has in adapting to his culture, and how this leads to the individual's inescapable difference from himself; the double life of who one wants to be, and to be seen as, and the other person one keeps on being. Freud would aspire to be an insider in the medical profession, with all the symbolic capital accruing from that position; while devising a medical treatment for the casualties of the culture he wanted to be a part of.

Freud's story of human development that he would begin to elaborate in his forties is all about the individual distinguishing himself from others through a series of necessary separations, the aim being a life of independent achievement. In his years at university, he becomes aware of the man he feels himself to be in relation to the man he wants to be; he begins to realize who he happens to be, who he is like, and who he would like to be like. And we can see his quest for intellectual fathers at the university was an implicit acknowledgement of his disappointment with his own father. It is as though he had felt so betrayed by his father's character that he needed to radically remake himself. To live out what he would later call a "family romance," the adopting of parents rather more suited to, rather more appropriate for, the extraordinary talents of their child. Great, cultured, mostly Protestant scientists rather than failed, uncultivated Jewish merchants.

It was during his medical studies in Vienna that the ground was laid, unbeknown to Freud, for his later groundbreaking work. In these years he was acquiring the tools—both a scientific methodology and a thorough grasp of evolutionary biology— that he could use, misuse, and improvise in his later work as a psychoanalyst. Everything that disrupted the culture—sexuality, violence, and the symptoms they became—psychoanalysis would at once reincorporate through coherent narrative, and describe as the necessary saboteurs of coherence and narrative. This would be Freud's paradoxical contribution to the science of human nature. A science of storytelling suspicious of narrative coherence, and ambivalent about scientific method. Freud's ambivalence, though, was the aftereffect of a scientific education that he valued for the rest of his life.

VIII

Describing what he would ultimately call the Unconscious was to be Freud's way of talking about why we can never settle down, and why we can't stop wanting to. But between 1875 and 1886, the years in which Freud studied at the University of Vienna, qualified as a doctor of medicine, and met and married Martha Bernays—Freud settled into the work of finding the work he wanted to do. The rites of passage, for an aspiring bourgeois man of his generation and class, were professional qualification and marriage. And in these years we see Freud's life as a double agent—that he would formalize in the role of the psychoanalyst who has to be both on the side of the patient's safety and security, and on the side of her disruptive desires—beginning to take shape. Emblematically he gets engaged to a solid, respectable, and cultured Jewish girl from a (mostly) reputable Orthodox family; and begins to treat mostly women disturbed and disabled by the waywardness of their desires and the bizarreness of their symptoms. He will experiment with, and briefly promote, cocaine, at once a stimulant and an anaesthetic. He will go to Paris and study with the great Charcot; but live, by his own account, an abstemious life in the "city of sin." And he will take his time to choose his profession, which ultimately he had to invent, partly because it involved this reconciling of irreconcilables. As though he was becoming a medium for the contradictions and conflicts of his time and place; and there was something heroic, something of a significant struggle in the being and the doing of this. Trying to become a reputable doctor of the disreputable; giving a scientific account of irrationality, of everything in the individual that both undermined scientific method and that made science itself sound like another neurotic structure; becoming the Jewish inventor of a science that he didn't want to be seen as that contradiction in terms, a Jewish science; inventing a discipline that, in its own terms, was both a symptom and a cure.

He took four years to marry the woman he was engaged to partly because he needed to establish himself professionally so he could afford, financially, to marry; but also because during this long engagement—from 1882, the year after he qualifies as a doctor of medicine, and 1886, the year in which he goes into private practice as a doctor of nervous diseases, and first uses the word "psychoanalysis" in print—he is doing two things that he would eventually describe as being at the heart of psychoanalytic theory and practice. He was overcoming, "working through," his resistances to what he was beginning to realize about the causes and meanings of certain kinds of human unhappiness; that their source was in the sexuality of early childhood. And he was doing a kind of protracted dream-work, composing unconsciously his education and his affinities, his childhood experience and his adult aspirations; formulating and forming his abiding concerns, which were also his desires for the future; beginning, that is to say, to find his questions, which involved realizing which were the answers that didn't work for him. One of Freud's questions was a simple one—how do people change each other? And he asked this ostensibly about parents and children and doctors and patients; and he saw the link between these relationships. But it was also a larger historical question about immigrants and their culture, about the fate of the Jews in Europe. And following on from this, How do we know what is a change for the better? would be the psychoanalytic question that would exercise him in his later years; a question, unsurprisingly, that his followers would have to take up, as it became increasingly clear that concepts of cure were created simply by consensus (concepts of cure are any given group's picture of what a life should be like). These questions would also be, more immediately, a way of working out what effect immensely influential teachers had had on him in the formative years of his university education.

IX

Four men were to dominate the early years of what became Freud's professional life—Ernst Brücke was his teacher at university, Charcot was his mentor and teacher for his months in Paris, and the other two, Josef Breuer and Wilhelm Fliess, would be his first two significant colleagues—and one woman, Martha Bernays, who became his wife. They provided him, after his family, with a kind of foundation—professional, financial, and emotional—from which he could discover what was preoccupying him. We have to imagine Freud as a student, a medical practitioner, and as a newly engaged young professional man, as someone not merely ambitious but casting around, like many young men before him, to crystalize, to formulate his preoccupations, out of what was already available in the culture. The boy with passionate interests—in literature and languages, in archaeology and ancient history—was trying to link these up with an available adult profession that he could earn his living by. And it was through these key relationships, perhaps more than many others, that Freud made himself a man about whom people would write biographies.

Freud, as I say, seems to have been very adept, throughout his adult life, at finding the people he needed to get him to the next chapter of his life. He was a man who had the courage of his affinities; when he was drawn to someone he pursued them passionately, as he did his future wife. And when he finished with them—as he did with Breuer and Fliess—he finished with them forever. And it was, of course, to be the unconsciousness of desire—our being driven in ineluctable directions—that Freud was also to explore in his later work; the attractions, and our resistance to these attractions, that shape our lives. All five of these people, in rather different ways, offered Freud an opening. He was gripped by something about them; and each of them backed his desire. They were on the side of his intent and divided curiosity. They saw something in him that he couldn't see himself. And this, too, was something Freud would try and formalize, and institutionalize in the role of the psychoanalyst. Psychoanalysis was to be Freud's enquiry into the uses (and misuses) of recognition, and into recognition as integral to development; how lives were shaped by what people wanted from each other, and could see in each other. But before the men we must turn to the woman who was to shape Freud's life definitively; and not simply or solely by creating the conditions, the family life, in which he could do his work. Freud, in fact, became a psychoanalyst because he had to get married.

X

Apart from Freud's protracted courtship of her, and their long life together, Freud's wife, Martha Bernays, has always been a rather shadowy presence in Freud's biography. In the story of Freud's life she becomes the taken-for-granted background, the essentially stable housekeeper and mother whose considerable work created the conditions—as the wives of such men are required to do—for the flourishing of genius. And yet nothing, in anything Freud wrote, could lead us to believe this. Indeed Freud's biographers, and possibly sometimes Freud himself, have colluded with what Freud took to be the primary human defense and therefore self-deception: the diminishing of the significance of the woman. So essential are the mother and the wife they must be kept out of the picture, their contribution clichéd and diminished, aided and abetted by the historical fact that their lives, at least until the twentieth century, are largely undocumented (the only real biography of Martha Freud, by Katja Behling, is a mere 173 pages for a life longer than her husband's). A thumbnail sketch is as misleading (and insulting) in its way, as the albeit vague acknowledgement that she must have been a very remarkable woman (which she clearly was). And of course given the nature of Freud's work—the confidentiality required, the privacy maintained—his wife would seem to be the ultimate shadowy and enigmatic presence in his life. But even though she is the absent center of the story of Freud's life, and much about her and her relationship with Freud cannot be known—and though she fades out or haunts the background of Freud biography—there are salient facts and impressions that are at least worth bearing in mind in a consideration of Freud's life. It does need to be born in mind that the consistent fact of Freud's adult life was his being married for fifty-three years to Martha Bernays.

Two of Martha Bernays's father's brothers were leading scholars; professor Jacob Bernays was a well-known classicist in Breslau, Bonn, and Heidelberg, and Michael Bernays was a professor of literature in Munich specializing in Goethe and Shakespeare. Freud's choice of wife, in other words, as Martha's biographer puts it, "was from the intellectual circles to which he himself aspired."[40] But she was also from other circles that he and she were keen to distance themselves from. When Martha was six her father was involved in what was called in the family "the insolvency incident" about which little is known except that the father was sent to prison, and the incident was apparently never discussed; nor, apparently, did Martha ever talk about her relationship with her father. Freud's father, we should remember, had been a largely unsuccessful businessman about whom there were "rumours," and his father's brother was sent to prison for counterfeit dealing (it was also said of Freud's half-brothers that their "dubious deals" in Manchester took care of "the family" but probably with "forged money and credit papers").[41] There were shady dealings in the recent histories of both families; and one of the effects of this was a drive, in both members of the young couple, for honest and honorable bourgeois respectability. The proximity of the cultured to the disreputable—how the illicit and the respectable were inextricable; the strange connection between Jews, dishonest money, and learning; survival and pleasure at all costs—would of course be the stuff of Freud's life that he would elaborate in his work.

But Martha was clearly a formidably intelligent and competent young woman. She had had an otherwise protected childhood in Hamburg and Vienna. In her family, her biographer tells us, "the Prussian virtues of decency, reliability, moral probity and perfectionism" were "the ethos to be emulated, and in this respect Martha was seen as very 'German.'"[42] But she was also remarkably independent-spirited, as many visitors to the Freud household would attest; "My mother," her daughter Anna once remarked, "observed no rules, she made her own rules."[43] Martha's parents were Orthodox Jews but Martha herself was also very interested in art and literature, which appealed to Freud—his first gift to her was *David Copperfield*— and every day at the beginning of their courtship Freud sent her a red rose with a poem in Latin or another foreign language. It was, that is to say, a literary and essentially romantic courtship; and we may wonder which of the women in *David Copperfield*—a story about a young English man making his way—Freud wanted Martha to be. And in what way, if at all, Freud identified with David Copperfield as a young man making his way.

Freud first met Martha in 1882 when she was twenty-one and Freud was nearly twenty-six; her father had recently died, and her family was financially insecure as a consequence. The couple met at Freud's family house, where she had been invited by Freud's sisters, who were friends of hers. It was apparently love at first sight; and the scene, as reconstructed by Freud in a letter to Martha of 1885, has a suggestive archness about it: it was, Freud wrote, "the first sight of a little girl sitting at a well-known long table talking so cleverly while peeling an apple with her delicate fingers" that had "disconcerted [him] lastingly."[44] A well-known story is knowingly being alluded to here, but it is possible that Freud experienced his desire for Martha as a concession, a yielding to something against his will, a fall of fatal and fateful consequences (which it was). It also makes the new couple the (transgressive) first parents of the human race, a not unambitious vision. Freud would spend much of his professional life listening to women talking so cleverly, revealing the intelligence of their speech, and wondering what women wanted (and, in the best and the worst sense, seeing women as little girls). Freud, of course, would take up in a new way the biblical connection between knowledge and sexuality. And the sense in which they were both forbidden because of the uncanny connection between them.

Freud apparently reminded Martha of her father—which, interestingly, he was pleased by—and two months after their first meeting they regarded themselves as secretly engaged.[45] For Freud this was something of a triumph, for two significant reasons. He had won what he called his "princess" from a family of greater social prestige than his own; and he had got a Jewish girl from an Orthodox family to marry a determinedly self-confessed atheist. During their long and mostly furtive engagement, in which Freud had trouble winning over Martha's domineering mother, Freud asked Martha to embroider for him two "votive tablets" to hang in his rather dingy lodgings in Vienna's General Hospital where he was training as a resident. The two inscriptions he asked for were "Travailler sans raisonner" (Work without reasoning) and "En cas de doute abstiens-toi" (When in doubt abstain). Perhaps Freud was having to remind himself not to be too curious. They were two of the young Freud's favourite mottos. The connections between work, reason, doubt, and abstinence were indeed to exercise Freud in the years ahead, abstinence and work seeming to characterize Freud's life at the time.

It was difficult for Freud and Martha to meet alone, and they communicated often by letter, Martha writing to a laboratory assistant at Ernst Brücke's institute of physiology where Freud worked. If Freud's partly secret unofficial "engagement" to Martha preoccupied Freud in these years he was also finding his feet professionally, having had the good fortune to work with the great Brücke. "In Ernst Brücke's physiological laboratory," Freud wrote in *An Autobiographical Study*, "I found rest and full satisfaction—and men, too, whom I could respect and take as my models: the great Brücke himself, and his assistants."[46] Freud's phrasing is suggestive here, the men with no mention of the woman, providing rest and full satisfaction. At its most minimal it is clear how important it was for Freud at this stage to find men, and men whom he could respect and take as models; men, that is, unlike his father. It was to be mostly fathers, not mothers, that Freud would use psychoanalysis to write about. Fathers made him fluent.

Brücke, Freud wrote, was "the greatest authority I ever met."[47] Brücke was a distinguished member of the Helmholtz School of Medicine, a group of remarkable German scientists, pioneers of a new science of rigorous materialism; and he was a German Protestant. Theirs was a vigorous critique of Romantic vitalism and mystical nature-worship, an interest only in what they called "the chemical-physical forces inherent in matter."[48] "Brücke and I pledged a solemn oath to put into effect this truth," as Emil Du Bois-Reymond, one member of the Helmholtz group, put it, "no other forces than the common physical-chemical ones are active within the organism. In those cases which cannot at the time be explained by these forces one has either to find the specific way or form of their action by means of the physical-mathematical method or to assume new forces equal in dignity to the chemical-physical forces inherent in matter, reducible to the force of attraction and repulsion."[49] The legacy of this method, of this hard-core Enlightenment science, in Freud's psychoanalysis, would be in his using the vocabulary of "force" and "energy" and "biological instinct" in his accounts of what he would call, in the same vein, the "psychic apparatus"; and a virulent distrust of faiths and superstitions.

Freud's faith was in empirical materialism; though his adolescent faith, we should remember, was in *Don Quixote*. The science Freud was studying was clearly a long way from his adolescent passion for ancient history and for literature; this is not the world of Shakespeare, of Cervantes, of Goethe, or, indeed, of David Copperfield. And this would be one of the rifts, one of the divided duties in Freud's sensibility that would lead to generative contradictions in the making of psychoanalysis as an "objective" study of subjectivity. Freud would not—unlike his later follower Lacan—use the "physical-mathematical method" in his psychoanalytic theorizing; but he would, as he often mentions—for example, in the *Three Essays on Sexuality*—assert that psychoanalytic research was waiting for confirmation from the "physical-chemical" sciences. And he would redescribe, in a language often more akin to literature, the "forces of attraction and repulsion" in his account of the erotic life, and indeed, of the death-drive. But he would also, as his psychoanalytic work progressed, want to separate psychoanalysis out from the physical sciences. "We have found it necessary," he would write in 1913, "to hold aloof from biological considerations during our psychoanalytic work and to refrain from using them for heuristic purposes so that we may not be misled in our impartial judgment of the psychoanalytic facts before us."[50] There were, in other words—extraordinary as it might seem, even to Freud himself—psychoanalytic facts that were not subject to biological description. Freud's youthful and lasting commitment to the physical sciences left him, as I say, with a profound ambivalence, a slightly baffled scepticism about the physical sciences. There was also, he would realize, something misleading about biological considerations alone, some things they couldn't account for. "Psychoanalysis, he would write later in 1916, "must keep itself free from any hypothesis that is alien to it, whether of an anatomical, chemical, or physiological kind."[51] If scientific hypotheses could be alien to psychoanalysis, which hypotheses were integral? If psychoanalysis wasn't a science, or wasn't only a science, what else was it? These were the questions that haunted Freud, and the profession he invented; and that emerged gradually out of his early training.

In Brücke's laboratory Freud studied the nerve cells of fish, and he published papers on the nerve cells of crayfish, and various other studies of the nervous system. According to Brücke Freud did outstanding work on the brain—publishing papers with titles like, "A Histological Method for the Study of Brain Tracts," and "A Case of Cerebral Hemorrhage"—and was an excellent teacher. Jonathan Lear has suggested that "were he living today Freud would likely be a neuroscientist and not a therapist of any kind," and this seems right.[52] But there may also have been something missing for Freud in the neurosciences that were just beginning to be at the center of the new medical research. Like many of today's psychoanalysts who are waiting around for neuroscientists to tell them the truth about human nature, Freud at this period of his life believed, as many people did (and do), that studying the brain and the nerves was at the cutting edge of scientific research. And yet, when he fell in love with Martha everything began to change. Freud began to experiment with cocaine, a different kind of experience from dissecting tissue, as indeed was falling in love. And he began an intimate, but apparently nonsexual, relationship with a slightly older attractive and talented colleague in Brücke's Institute, Ernst Fleischl von Marxow, who became a drug addict that

Freud tried to help. It wasn't that passionate relationships were displacing Freud's interest in his work—his work seems to have been an unfailing object of desire for him—but that two things seemed to happen together. Freud was becoming more absorbed by the attractions and repulsions between people than by the workings of the brain; and most pressingly of all, if he was to marry the woman he now loved he would need to do more lucrative work (the erotic motive, in this instance, being the precondition for the economic motive). He would need to become a medical doctor, and so a therapist of some sort, in immediate contact with people wanting help.

"The turning point came in 1882," he wrote in *An Autobiographical Study*, when Brücke, "my teacher for whom I felt the highest possible esteem, corrected my father's generous improvidence by strongly advising me, in view of my bad financial position, to abandon my theoretical career. I followed his advice, left the physiological laboratory and entered the General Hospital."[53] A good fatherlike figure replaces a bad—unprotecting, unproviding, unstimulating—father (in the English translation, at least, the phrase "theoretical career" has a certain resonance). "In a certain sense I nevertheless remained faithful," Freud wrote in his *Autobiographical Study*, and we should take him at his word, "to the line of work upon which I had originally started" in Brücke's laboratory; and he went on writing throughout the 1880s research papers on histology and neuroscience.[54] But like much else Freud immersed himself in he would transform what he had learned, or repudiate it; and he would transform what he had learned about the neurosciences through the prism of his doubts about science, and his discoveries about the unconscious and sexuality.

Freud would later claim that his time in Brücke's laboratory was the happiest period of his life; and so he left it with relative ease for a professional life of live exchanges with real people. Instead of dissection and research there would be conversation and treatment. But Freud was to continue his interest in fundamental things, in what makes us who and what we are. Human nature was to be studied also through words not only through cells, through meaning-making rather than brain-functioning. Freud would not, unlike some of his latter-day followers, return, so to speak, to the brain. He wanted a different kind of life; and he wanted to do a different kind of writing. His scientific training, his desire for science, never left him; but it was complicated by other desires, not least the implicit question, What was the desire for science, for scientific method and enquiry, a desire for? If love came before science—was the precondition for it as it was in the individual's development—what was the link between love and science? In his 1910 paper on Leonardo da Vinci Freud would write about this explicitly, about what it was about Leonardo's childhood that caused him to, as Freud puts it, "sublimate his libido into the urge to know."[55] Science comes late in the day to everyone, after the instinctual vicissitudes of childhood, after the love of children and parents.

In retrospect we can say that Freud needed his early passions for ancient history, for literature, and then for the new scientific method of his time to manage the full complexity of his experience; the anticipation of adulthood—the anticipation of sexuality and of earning money, of earning an adult living. These gave him a language, a way of thinking, for this transitional period; and this disparate language never left him. Freud would become the most literary of psychoanalysts, with a lifelong interest in ancient history, and a lifelong question about scientific method as the best, or the only, model for psychoanalysis. But once he fell in love, however secretly, with Martha something about medicine—and not simply or solely that it was a viable and prestigious way of supporting a wife and family—became the life Freud wanted to lead. And we should remember here Freud's subsequent doubts and misgivings about himself as a doctor; his resistance to what was to be a life in medicine and the legacy of his ambivalence in the history of psychoanalysis in which the question has always been, Is psychoanalysis a medical specialty? Freud becoming a doctor in these years was at once against the grain, and entirely of a piece with his interest in what was human about human nature. But we should think of Freud's becoming a doctor as an enigmatic demand he made on himself at a significant point in his life; and wonder what he wanted from the profession of medicine, and that he believed he would not be able to get from any other occupation.

3

Freud Goes to Paris

Freud's eye was the microscope of potency.
—Wallace Stevens, "Mountains Covered with Cats"

TO UNDERSTAND WHY Freud went to Paris in 1885 to study
with the great French physician Jean-Martin Charcot, the so-
called Napoleon of the neuroses, we need to understand the
difference between a nerve cell and a hysterical woman; and we
need to wonder what it might have been that Freud was becoming interested in, as a twenty-nine-year-old aspiring neuroanatomist, by choosing Charcot as his teacher and hysteria as
his preferred neurosis, the neurosis he would begin by specializing in? What it was that was shifting Freud's attention away
from the study of neuroanatomy as the study of cells and tissue
towards the links between neurology and self-presentation; away
from the mechanisms of the body towards the living and speaking person. Freud, of course, at this period of his life having a

fiancée, and wanting a profession; having an interest in medicine but coming to study in late nineteenth century Paris, notoriously the city of the senses.

Freud, though he was very lonely at first and considered coming home, went to the theatre—got cheap seats, "really shameful pigeon-hole loges"[1] for plays by Molière, for Beaumarchais's *Le Mariage de Figaro*—went to galleries, saw the sights but determinedly resisted the supposed immorality of the French. "As you see my heart is German," he wrote to Martha, "provincial, and in any case did not come along with me."[2] And yet when Freud went to see the great actress Sarah Bernhardt perform in Paris he was struck, as he wrote to his fiancée, Martha, by "her intimate endearing voice . . . every inch of this little figure was alive and bewitching . . . her caressing and pleading and embracing the postures she assumes, the way she wraps herself around a man."[3] So exciting was this for Freud that, as he writes, "I again had to pay for this pleasure with an attack of migraine."[4] Whether or not he experienced it as an infidelity, something that he had to confess to Martha, the experience at the theatre was of a piece with his experience of being a student in Paris. It was seduction, enchantment, the apparently irresistible—the immediate and unaccountable effect that bodies can have on each other, the promise of pleasure— that Freud was both resisting and thinking about. And that was giving him a headache. This was almost surprising for Freud, a rather studious and austere young man, this preoccupation; though hardly surprising for a man of his age leaving home properly for the first time. In Paris there were women, hysterical or otherwise, performing or not; there were performing hypnotists, both entertainers and genuine medical doctors, and there was the great Charcot who combined all these elements in his extraordinary character. In Paris as a student Freud was finding the differences between the official life and the unofficial life beginning to blur. There were bodies as informative objects, the bodies of anatomy and physiology, objects of scientific interest. And there were bodies as evocative subjects and objects, of scientific and of more than scientific interest.

Freud, we might say, was becoming interested in credulousness, and the connections between credulousness and desire; he was becoming more and more interested in what drew people to each other, in what it is that makes us believe, and believe in, other people and in ourselves. He was more and more preoccupied by what the critic Richard Poirier calls "the performing self," in which the individual, "shaping a self out of the materials in which it is immersed,"[5] makes their presence felt: performance, Poirier writes, "is an exercise of power, a very curious one," that commands assent, and often desire. "Out of an accumulation of secretive acts," Poirier writes, "emerges at last a form that presumes to compete with reality itself for control of the minds exposed to it."[6] Through the performing self every force evolves a form, or many forms. Both Charcot and the hysterics he treated could be said to be competing with reality itself for control of the minds exposed to them, through the forming and fashioning of their particular selves; though people often didn't believe in hysterics, called them "malingerers" and "actresses," whereas they did, for a time, believe in Charcot as a clinician and diagnostician. Both Charcot and his hysterics were extraordinary performers, the power they had over their audiences at once enigmatic and stimulating. But Charcot had succeeded where the hysteric had failed. This power was something the young Freud wanted, and his wanting took the characteristic form of a wanting to understand and explain.

"I consider it a great misfortune," he wrote from Paris to his fiancée, Martha, "that nature has not granted me that indefinite something which attracts people. I believe it is this lack more than any other which has deprived me of a rosy existence."[7] Charcot had this "indefinite something," and hysteria, one might say, was an attempted cure for its absence. Freud, at this stage in his life, was suffering from what psychoanalysts would eventually call a split identification. He identified with the hysterics as the discarded, the thwarted, and the misunderstood, people with baffled desire and stalled ambition; people who, not unlike Jews, made people inordinately suspicious (hysteria was referred to by a colleague of Charcot's as "a wastepaper basket of medicine where one throws otherwise unemployed symptoms"); and he identified with Charcot as a man he would like to become, and as a man very unlike his own father—the educated, cultured doctor who took hysterics seriously and engaged with their confounding and confounded predicament, a doctor who was rich and influential (Freud, it should be noted, was oppressed, during his five months in Paris, by his family's worsening poverty).[8] Charcot was one of the most famous physicians in Europe—scientists and artists flocked to his informal "receptions" at his grand house, and to his lectures and demonstrations at the Salpêtrière, the hospital that he referred to as a "great emporium of human misery . . . a sort of living pathological museum."[9] He was the promoter and curator of some of the most disturbed patients in Paris, the impresario of this strange and infamous institution. He was the great describer and classifier of hysterical symptoms, but ultimately committed to the hereditary and organic basis of hysteria. It would be the inherited, organic nature of hysteria that Freud would eventually contest. But not before becoming thoroughly awestruck by Charcot's character both as a physician and as a teacher. In his obituary of Charcot in 1893 Freud wrote of "the magic that emanated from his looks and from his voice, to the kindly openness that characterised his manner . . . the willingness with which he put everything at the disposal of his pupils, and his life-long loyalty to them."[10] We have to imagine Freud in Paris in these months above all as a devoted and diligent student of his so-called Master. And in these crucial months Freud would begin to move over from an interest in neuropathology to a lifelong

passion for psychology, and psychosexuality; for the performances of the self.

Freud would learn from Charcot about observation, about
repeated attentiveness to nuance and detail; but it would be
what Poirier calls "the accumulation of secretive facts" that,
like a work of art becomes a form—a symptom, a turn of phrase,
a character trait—that were beginning to fascinate Freud, and
that would preoccupy him on his return to Vienna. Forms that
as Poirier suggests "presume to compete with reality itself for
control of the minds exposed to it." These forms, both persua-
sive and spellbinding, describe well the power of hysterical symptoms, the power of Charcot's performances, and, ultimately, the
power of what would become Freud's psychoanalysis. There
was to be a dramatic difference, in both senses, between the
histology labs in Vienna in which Freud had conducted his
neurological research and what one historian has called Charcot's "hysterical circus," in which, among other things, Charcot
would demonstrate the workings of hysterical symptoms with a
patient in front of an invited audience. It was rather macabre
theatre under the rubric of science.[11] Freud went to Paris to
continue his researches into neuroanatomy, but he ended up
studying Charcot. And in this formative period between 1884
and 1894 of meetings (and collaborations) with remarkable
men—Charcot, Fliess, and Breuer—it was Charcot who was to
have the greatest influence on Freud's life and work. He would
name his first son Martin after Charcot, and he would, for the
rest of his life, have a portrait of Charcot in his study, even after
much of Charcot's work had been discredited, not least by
Freud himself.

Freud went to Paris on a government-sponsored traveling
fellowship open to junior doctors at Vienna General Hospital
backed by his mentor Brücke—"Brücke's passionate interces-
sion . . . had caused a general sensation," his friend Fliess told
him[12]—to study with the great neurologist. But the first reality

Freud had presumed to compete with was the reality of Charcot's popularity. Freud, though, was adept, at getting the attention, and the backing, of the men he was drawn to. "I became
a student at the Salpêtrière," he writes in *An Autobiographical
Study*,

> but, as one of the crowd of foreign visitors, I had little atten-
> tion paid to me to begin with. One day in my hearing Char-
> cot expressed his regret that since the war he had heard
> nothing from the German translator of his lectures; he went
> on to say that he would be glad if someone would undertake
> to translate the new volume of his lectures into German. I
> wrote to him and offered to do so.[13]

Freud's offer was accepted, and Freud became a closer
colleague of Charcot's, visiting his home and family; and his
translation—appropriately enough for a favored son—came
out before the original French edition, Charcot sending Freud
a bound set of his collected works by way of thanks. It seems, at
least in retrospect, an emblematic Freudian scene. Freud, the
future analyst, overhears something—as opposed to hearing
something addressed to him—about someone's frustration. He
intervenes and the person's words are at last in circulation.
"Translation" would be one of Freud's analogies for the workings of the psyche, and for the task of the psychoanalyst.

There were, Freud recounts, two things Charcot said to him
that he never forgot—that are linked, though not by Freud—
and that he refers to in *On the History of the Psycho-Analytic Movement*, written in 1914, nearly thirty years after his time in Paris
(the *History* has as its epigraph, perhaps not incidentally, "Fluc-
tuat nec mergitur" (It is tossed by the waves but does not sink)
which is written on the coat of arms of the city of Paris: as
though in Freud's mind the history of the psychoanalytic movement began in Paris). The first comment of Charcot's that Freud
quotes was made at one of Charcot's "evening receptions," and

was once again something overheard by Freud. A case was being discussed of a young couple, the woman "a severe sufferer," presumably of hysteria, and the man "either impotent or exceedingly awkward."[14] "I heard Charcot repeating," Freud writes, "Mais, dans ces pareils c'est toujours la chose genitale, toujours . . . toujours . . . toujours" (But in this sort of case it's always a question of the genitals—always . . . always . . . always).[15] "I was almost paralysed with amazement," Freud writes, "and said to myself, 'Well, if he knows that, why does he never say so?'"[16] Charcot knew, in other words, as Freud was to know, that it, hysterical misery, was always about sexuality, about how and if the genitals get together (though Freud was to extend the genital area to the whole body, and so make sexuality less normatively heterosexual). Charcot's remark, Freud notes knowingly, was, as he says, "soon forgotten; brain anatomy and the experimental induction of hysterical paralyses absorbed all my interest."[17] Soon forgotten but never forgotten.

The other memorable thing that Freud learned from Charcot was about looking, which would become for Freud one of the more important sexual (and sexualisable) activities. "I learnt," Freud writes, "to restrain speculative tendencies and to follow the unforgettable advice of my master, Charcot: to look at the same things again and again until they themselves begin to speak."[18] As a scientist Freud privileged observation over speculation; as a psychoanalyst he would privilege listening over looking, and he would realize that observation was always formed and forced by unconscious speculation; the innocent ear heard nothing. In a sense Freud was to look at the genitals, at the sexual, to let it speak. But we need to notice here Charcot and Freud's phrasing—looking attentively, repeatedly, lets the object speak; it reveals itself through the quality of the attention given to it. The empirical is the route to the verbal. The project is to let things, and people—and the impersonal things of which people consist—be evocative such that they seem to speak for themselves. But when they speak, and when they don't, it is always the genital thing. What Freud learnt from Charcot was that sexuality was the thing, and that the method of informed, repeated, observation was to let things speak, and to avoid speaking on their behalf. In psychoanalysis Freud would let people speak, but be speaking on their behalf when he thought he knew what they were talking about. Science was the kind of knowledge that allowed scientists to speak on other people's behalf, to know better. The doctor knows more about the patient's body than the patient does, but there are many ways in which the patient knows and experiences his body in ways the doctor can't. It was this essential perplexity that crystalized in Freud through observing the spectacular Charcot, and that would be the heart of the matter for psychoanalysis. Do psychoanalysts know what people are talking about or just know how to let people speak for themselves?

It was from Paris that Freud wrote to Martha that he had "now overcome the love for science in so far as it stood between us, and that I want nothing but you,"[19] as though the lover and the scientist might somehow be at odds with each other; or even that science was an obstacle to love, a resistance to it. Certainly Freud at this period in his life was using Charcot to redescribe science (and scientists) for himself; or rather, he was wanting a new picture of what science and scientists could be, one that would eventually suit the psychoanalyst. For Freud Charcot was the scientist as artist, a paradoxical person. A great neurologist who would quote Dante or Virgil, a doctor whose work artists and writers were intrigued by.

Indeed there were two other things that had struck Freud about his "master"—he often reminded him of an artist, and he was radically skeptical of theory, of the misleading omniscience of the forms and formulations that scientific research was given to ("Theory is good," he once famously said in a lecture, "but it doesn't prevent things from existing").[20] He was a man, Freud wrote, who "when the present state of science did not allow him to know, was able to make a good guess. . . . Each of his lectures was a little work of art . . . it was perfect in form and made such an impression that for the rest of the day one could not get the sound of what he had said out of one's ears."[21] It was the guesswork and the artwork that haunted Freud. Psychoanalysis was to be the art and science of guesswork. After all, the analyst and the patient can only say what occurs to them.

Charcot was certainly not the kind of scientist that Freud was used to; he was charismatic, curious, interested in other people. In short, he was someone who was enjoying himself. He was, Freud wrote to Martha—stressing the hedonism of the man he spent seventeen of his twenty weeks in Paris with, attending his lectures, ward rounds, and seminars—"like a worldly priest from whom one expects a ready wit and an appreciation of good living . . . I was very much impressed by his brilliant diagnosis and the lively interest he took in everything, so unlike what we are accustomed to from our great men with their veneer of distinguished superficiality."[22] Or, as the Goncourt brothers put it in their diary, "As a scientist Charcot was a mixture of genius and charlatan."[23] Words, of course, that would be used about Freud. For "mixture of genius and charlatan" we should read, "mixture of scientist and performing artist." And we need to remember this for the light it sheds on Freud's future, and reputation, and on the reputation of the profession he invented with its strange mixture of private theatricality and empirical method, of powerful conviction and radical uncertainty about its own status. And its subtle asceticising of the erotic.

He "was not a reflective man, not a thinker: he had the nature of an artist,"[24] Freud wrote of his "Master" Charcot who had become in a very short time, a new kind of man, a new kind of medical doctor, for Freud to emulate. To begin with, as a young foreign student who barely spoke the language, Freud had felt lost in Paris, amazed and threatened—Paris, he wrote, was "magic," but "a vast overdressed Sphinx who gobbles up every foreigner unable to solve her riddles"[25]—but his relationship with Charcot changed everything. Always Oedipus, Freud had, through Charcot's effect, solved the riddle of the Sphinx that was Paris; or rather, the riddles not the riddle because Paris was an even more demanding Sphinx than the one Oedipus had to deal with; it had asked him so many questions that he would spend his life in psychoanalysis trying to answer. And "an overdressed Sphinx" is an image worth thinking about. "I think I am changing a great deal," he wrote to Martha. "Charcot, who is one of the greatest of physicians and a man whose common sense is touched by genius, is simply uprooting my aims and opinions. I sometimes come out of his lectures as though I were coming out of Notre Dame, with a new idea of perfection."[26] This was to be the effect Freud and the psychoanalysis he invented was to have; it was common sense touched by genius that would significantly uproot people's aims and opinions. And more strangely Freud compares Charcot to a medieval cathedral named after a woman.

The Parisians, Freud wrote to Martha, "are people given to psychical epidemics, historical mass convulsions, and they haven't changed since Victor Hugo wrote *Notre Dame*. To understand Paris this is the novel you must read; although everything in it is fiction, one is convinced of its truth."[27] Freud himself had suffered some kind of psychical epidemic, some convulsion working in Paris with Charcot ("He exhausts me," Freud wrote of Charcot, "when I come away from him I no longer have any desire to work at my own silly things . . . no-one else has ever affected me in the same way").[28] We can only speculate now why Hugo's novel was for Freud the key to Paris, or perhaps to his own experience of being in Paris: the overt Romanticism of the book with its explicit commitment to freer forms of thought might have appealed to Freud; Quasimodo, the hunchback that the book is famous for, was certainly a character who, as Freud said of himself, had not been granted "that indefinite something which attracts people," so the beauty and the beast element of the story could have been something that Freud identified with. But it is a story, above all, about a fatefully attractive woman, as psychoanalysis would be. And like psychoanalysis—the fiction Freud was soon to start writing—everything in the novel was fiction though one was convinced of its truth. To be interested in the psychological rather than the neurological was patently to be interested in fictions as truths. And for the hysteric, as for the psychoanalyst treating her, Freud would find, so much would depend on these distinctions between truth and fiction, between fantasy and reality.

Before Freud had gone to Paris he had become friendly with an older colleague, Josef Breuer. Breuer was a Viennese Jewish doctor and the son of a "progressive" scholar and teacher of Judaism; his father, Breuer wrote—unlike Freud's father—"belonged to that generation of Jews who were the first to emerge from the intellectual ghetto into the free atmosphere of western civilization."[29] Fourteen years older than Freud, he had also studied under Brücke, and was already a distinguished physiologist when Freud met him in the late 1870s. They became close friends and colleagues—Freud was a frequent visitor to the Breuers' house, and named his eldest daughter Mathilde after Breuer's wife—but Breuer also became the younger Freud's sponsor, lending him money and referring him patients. "The ever-loyal Breuer," as Freud referred to him to Martha—a portent of his future disloyalty to Breuer—was a support and an inspiration at a time when Freud was struggling.[30] Struggling to make a career and, after his return from Paris, struggling as a newly married man, to make a name for himself. On his return from Paris in 1886 Freud finally married Martha, but in the aftermath, in the fallout, of his meeting with Charcot. The Freud who apparently embraced Breuer on his return, the young

Freud not being notably an effusively affectionate person, was a man of changed and changing ambitions. If you put wishing at the heart of human development, as Freud was to do within the next decade of his work, you make extravagant ambition your theme. Hysterical symptoms—and later sexuality and the death-drive—are forms of ambition. It was through his work with Breuer that Freud would begin to formulate his new questions: what was the hysteric's ambition, and what was the ambition of the doctor in treating her?

Like Charcot, Breuer was a cultured and curious doctor, a great conversationalist on a wide range of topics, but unlike Charcot he was a modest man ("With all his great intellectual gifts," Freud would write, giving us a clue about his own aims and aspirations, "there was nothing Faustian in his nature").[31] Though a successful and highly regarded doctor in Vienna he had not been able to make a career within the official institutions; partly, he believed, because of his religion. As Freud tried to establish himself in private practice—Freud had been made a *Privatdozent* (unpaid lecturer) at the Vienna medical school, but this was status without income—Breuer was his most important ally. "He became my friend and helper in my difficult circumstances," Freud wrote in his *Autobiographical Study* over thirty years after his relationship with Breuer had ended. "We grew accustomed to share all our scientific interests with each other. In this relationship the gain was naturally mine."[32] The gain was naturally his, and Freud would be guilty for many years about what he had gained from Breuer. Between his return from Paris in 1886, and the publication in 1900, after his protracted self-analysis, of *The Interpretation of Dreams*, Freud would "work through" the dramatic effect of Charcot in his relationships, both personal and professional, with Breuer, and with the German nose-and-throat specialist Wilhelm Fliess. The wildly speculative Fliess would gradually take over from the "ever-loyal," more cautiously respectable (and clearly loveable) Breuer. By the turn of the century Freud had broken with both men after an initial passionate attachment (more passion with Fliess, more attachment to Breuer). But it was his relationship with Breuer, and Breuer's involvement in the inventions of psychoanalysis, that Freud would guiltily return to in his later accounts.

Hysteria, in all its melee of bizarre physical symptoms—the convulsions, the paralyses, the tics and twitches and fervent inhibitions of physical functions—seemed to be about the strange effects people in intimate relationships can have on each other; about the desires and longings stirred, the conflicts that ensue, and the self-cures for these desires and conflicts called neurotic symptoms. This, at least, was what Freud and Breuer thought they were beginning to discover. Charcot had said that it was always the genital thing. Freud would write in *The Sexual Aetiology of The Neuroses* of 1898—four years after Freud and Breuer had published their own conclusions in *Studies on Hysteria*—that "so far as the theory of the sexual aetiology of neurasthenia is concerned, there are no negative cases . . . neurasthenia is one of those affections which anyone may easily acquire without having any hereditary taint."[33] Freud would have to go through his studies of hysteria with Breuer, to reconfirm Charcot's point; but he would radically redescribe sexuality as not literally the genital thing, but as the word for the desiring individual's experience of growing up in a family (the individual surviving because he wants from others: sexuality being of a piece with this and not a new thing that starts at puberty). And Freud would also, through his work with Breuer, disconfirm Charcot's conviction that hysteria was hereditary and organically based. Hysteria was a solution, by way of apparently unintelligible physical symptoms, to something from the past, but from the personal past; and a solution available to everyone, part of a more democratic toolkit for living in modern societies. (For contemporary antisemites, of course, Judaism similarly was itself a hereditary degenerative condition.) Indeed hysterical symptoms, as described by Breuer and Freud, began to sound more and more like cultural artifacts, devices invented to make family life and the growing up it involved bearable, rather than malfunctions of an otherwise well-functioning organism. Out of his intimacies with men, with whom he discussed women and children; and more importantly, through his intimacy with his wife and growing family—between 1887 and 1895 the Freuds had their six children—Freud evolved a theory about intimacy; a theory that linked memory and sex with the bizarre phenomena of hysterical symptoms. Freud was telling himself a story about what he was going through. About how the past keeps catching up with people in the sexuality of their lives. And about what, if anything, knowledge has to do with, and can do for, the sufferings of appetite.

"With Freud's own writings," the philosopher Alisdair MacIntyre writes, "it is continually necessary for the reader to turn back from the theorising to the case-histories, from the inflated conceptual schemes to the revealing clinical detail or other shrewd empirical observations; and it is in such observations that in the end the evidence for the truth or the falsity of psychoanalytic claims must be found."[34] One of the things that had interested Freud about classical antiquity—and that would interest him about childhood—was the paucity of evidence, and the vivid imaginings the lack of evidence produced. And compared with the sheer volume of Freud's conceptual scheming, inflated or otherwise, there is a notable paucity of clinical material in Freud's work. This crucial period of Freud's work, between 1885 and 1900—in which Freud moves from writing neurology to psycho-neurology, and in which psychoanalytic claims start to be made—begins with a set of case histories co-authored with Breuer, *Studies on Hysteria*, which to Freud sound, ominously, like short stories, like imaginative speculation; and so raise the question, as they clearly did in Freud's mind, of what the criteria were going to be for the truth or falsity of psychoanalytic claims; the hysteric, like the analyst having to struggle to be believed. "I have not always been a psychotherapist," Freud writes ruefully in the *Studies on Hysteria*, alerting the reader, and the reader who is himself, to an anxiety about his affinities and allegiances:

> Like other neuropathologists I was trained to employ local diagnoses and electro-prognosis, and it still strikes me as strange that the case-histories I write should read like short stories and that, as one might say, they lack the serious stamp of science.[35]

Were there other serious stamps, than the serious stamp of science? And was a serious stamp required, and if so, why? These are Freud's vexing questions at the inception of psychoanalysis.

In the years in which Freud was building up a private practice and writing what would eventually be published as *Studies on Hysteria* he had six children under the age of eight; between the time of their marriage and the publication of Freud's book Martha was almost continually pregnant and nursing. Writing and clinical work in these years were not, one assumes, the only things happening in Freud's life. It was not, in other words, as Freud has helped us to say, accidental that Freud was studying the rigors of family life while he was living them. And when people have children, of course, they remember their own childhoods and the parenting they did and did not have. Hysteria, Freud was realizing through his work with Breuer, was a way of surviving modern family life; though not, in its worst cases, a way of reproducing it. Critics of the family were called hysterics.

Before Freud had gone to Paris Breuer had told him of a remarkable woman—Bertha Pappenheim, known to psychoanalytic history by the unfortunate name Anna O. (Anna was the name of Freud's youngest daughter, and "o" has its associations)—that he had treated unsuccessfully. Interestingly Freud had tried, and failed, to interest Charcot in this case when he was in Paris. Bertha Pappenheim was a young woman who came from an Orthodox Jewish family, but was more interested in the arts than in religion (the parallels with Breuer and Freud are patent). In 1880 her father had fallen ill and she began to experience bizarre and disturbing symptoms while she nursed him: she developed anaesthesias, spasms, deafness, absences, paralyses. She could no longer speak in her mother tongue, but communicated fluently in English. She was, she told Breuer, split into "two selves, a real one and an evil one."[36] When her father died she got worse, becoming suicidal, and would only be fed by her "beloved" Breuer. Breuer though, was not mystified by the range or the severity of her symptoms; these were identifiable, by this time, as an albeit extreme case of hysteria, and he treated her accordingly. He tried hypnotizing her, which was now part of at least one of the new treatments for hysteria, it having been discovered—and this was something that, unsurprisingly, had interested Freud—that hysterical symptoms could be both induced and alleviated by enquiry under hypnosis. If hysterical symptoms could be conjured up by words, it suggested that they were at least partly psychological. And hypnosis itself might be an unusually revealing picture of the kind of effect people had on each other. Whether we believe (and desire and act) because we are hypnotized, or whether we are hypnotized because we believe Freud was to study as the question of transference; the unusually intriguing and disturbing question of how people influence people, something lived in the family, and examined in what became psychoanalytic treatment. But one of the many interesting things about Bertha was that she didn't need to be hypnotized because she seemed to already be, intermittently, in a kind of hypnotic trance. Breuer discovered, led by her, that if he just let her speak her fantasies through what she called "the talking cure," it began to alleviate her symptoms. The relief, though, was only temporary. By the time she was finally hospitalized by Breuer she was a morphine addict. She would eventually become, not incidentally, a pioneering feminist and social worker in Germany, though she was apparently to have no relationships with men in her long life, nor did she have children. She was, in a sense, the first of many failed cases in what would become psychoanalysis, in which the doctor got as much if not more than the patient. What Breuer learned from the case, and that Freud would eventually elaborate—the work coming to its first conclusion in the *Studies on Hysteria*—was the value of a treatment that was essentially collaborative. Bertha, Breuer noted, was "completely unsuggestible; she was only influenced by arguments, never by mere assertions."[37] She taught Breuer how she wanted, in both senses, to be treated. She didn't want the treatment to replicate the preconditions for her suffering; her father was an Orthodox Jew who founded a synagogue in Vienna, and demanded that his daughter become a dedicated Jewish wife. Breuer did not make her submit to a regime of treatment. Freud's psychoanalysis would be a collaborative treatment about the failures of collaboration in a person's life. By letting Bertha speak Breuer could hear and read her symptoms as disguised representations of memory and desire. Bertha was encoding in her symptoms the conflicts evoked in her by the demands of her family, what she wanted as opposed to what the family wanted from her. She was trying to make a future for herself out of her (Orthodox) Jewish past. At its most minimal Breuer took her seriously, which meant taking her to be someone who was trying to do something of value to and for herself; something that finally could only be done through the agonizing cartoon of her symptoms. Symptoms Breuer could not exempt himself from being somehow involved in.

Freud's relationship with Breuer was punctuated, we might say, by his virtual infatuation with Charcot. Anna O. became, unlike the four other main cases described in *Studies On Hysteria*, infatuated with Breuer. It was the way in which people captured each other's imaginations—the defining irrationality that people evoked in each other, the secret communications between people—that fascinated Freud; and that would be the founding perplexity of psychoanalysis. Through psychoanalysis Freud found a language to describe the ways in which men and women drove each other crazy; and the ways in which this craziness, this putative irrationality, was measured against a no less questionable rationality ("We must never let our poor neurotics drive us crazy," Freud would write ominously to Jung in 1911). Every culture had its own official consensus about what were acceptable forms of exchange—of food, words, sex, and money—between people. Psychoanalysis made it all too clear to Freud—though he would not have put it like this—that the compromised forms of exchange were called symptoms. It was as though, through encouraging the patient to say whatever came to mind, something barely containable, something in excess of scientific description, was being disclosed about modern people. That their official development was radically at odds with their unofficial development.

There was a contagion of feeling between people that was volatile, extravagant, and unpredictable; and that could only be officially acknowledged by being pathologized in the supposedly masterful language of science. Hysterical symptoms, like falling in love—and, indeed, like hero worship—revealed the demonic power of what had once been called the imagination. Freud, understandably, wanted the psychoanalyst—and, indeed, himself—to be rather more like Sancho Panza than like Don Quixote. But everything in the psychoanalysis he invented would show him why and how they were inextricable. "When I was a young student," Freud wrote in 1923, "the desire to read the immortal Don Quixote in the original of Cervantes led me to learn, untaught, the lovely Castilian tongue."[38] Such was the desire of Freud's youth. And through psychoanalysis he did indeed continue to immortalize Don Quixote. A story, we should remember, of two men; and of what they were capable of doing together in the service of a woman. One of them, of course— Don Quixote—dominated to the point of madness by a fictional past.

4

Freud Begins to Dream

Empirical knowledge, like its sophisticated extension
science, is rational, not because it has a foundation,
but because it is a self-correcting enterprise
which can put any claim into jeopardy,
though not all at once.
—Wilfrid Sellars, *Empiricism and the
Philosophy of Mind*

"DARING AND UNRESTRAINED IMAGINATION always stirred
Freud," Ernest Jones wrote. "It had captured him with Fliess.
. . . It was an integral part of his own nature to which he rarely
gave full rein . . . the sight of this unchecked imagination in
others was something Freud could seldom resist."[1] Daring
and unrestrained imagination had, of course, captured Freud
in Charcot and, indeed, in the hysterical patients who were
becoming Freud's clinical specialty. And Wilhelm Fliess, the

eccentric ear, nose, and throat specialist from Berlin, became Freud's next wayward "genius" after Charcot, the man who, as he put it in a letter, gave "meaning" to his life. "It is primarily through your example," Freud wrote, "that intellectually I gained the strength to trust my judgement."[2] Through Fliess, it would be truer to say, Freud began, unwittingly, to trust his own daring and unrestrained imagination. Jones intimates, perhaps rightly, that this was a part of himself that Freud was troubled (and tempted) by, and delegated to others; a part of himself that he had found, in his youth, in Cervantes and Goethe and Shakespeare, but not always in his revered teachers at medical school.

It is in these years of his close relationship with Wilhelm Fliess that Freud began to allow himself a more wildly speculative self; the respectable scientific doctor becoming also something akin to a visionary artist. "The normative Freud," as Mark Edmundson puts it—"a therapist whose objective it is to acquaint his patients and his readers with the causes of their sufferings and to show them the way to psychological health"—is joined by the Freud who is, in Edmundson's useful words, "best conceived of as a Romantic writer . . . whose objective is symbolic self-reinvention," a "self-creator [who] places very little stock in the normative standards of the devoted therapist. His objective is originality." Unlike the more reassuring normative therapist—thoroughly au fait with the norms of psychological health: a man who knows what a cure is, that is, who knows the official version of the good life—the Romantic Freud aspires "to displace his culture's favoured modes of description and explanation for nearly everything that matters in human experience."[3] Freud's struggle to make and to keep psychoanalysis scientifically legitimate, that would begin in these years, was, among other things, a way of acknowledging that his disturbing discoveries were difficult to contain; scientific method was a reassurance as Freud embarked on the finding of forms—the making of sentences, the forging and forcing of analogies—for what was beginning to occur to him. It is partly through his relationship with Fliess, and partly through the rigors and rememberings of family life, that the young Freud with a passion for literature and archaeology begins to catch up with the aspiring neurologist to invent a new kind of person, the psychoanalyst; and a new kind of double act, the analyst and the psychoanalytic patient. The analyst is a doctor but sounds like a short story writer: a person who, in treating patients begins to realize that he is a patient himself. A person who in joining the medical profession begins to estrange himself from it. A person without a discernible tradition to align himself with. A person who assimilates and refuses assimilation *at the same time.*

Both Jones, the psychoanalyst and younger contemporary of Freud, and Edmundson, the modern literary critic, are reminding us, in their different ways, that there are at least two Freuds, or at least that it has been convenient to describe him in this way. But it is in these years that the two Freuds come to light, wrestling like Jacob and the angel, but they are also, like Jacob and the angel, a productive couple. And these two Freuds are not simply, in the now-clichéd terms we have inherited from the nineteenth century, the scientist and the artist, or the secular and the religious; or indeed the cultural critic and the doctor. Rather we could say that in Freud we can see the confluence of these disciplines and traditions beginning to work themselves out. And it is in these years, at the very end of the century, in which Freud begins to let his mind wander—and invents that most paradoxical thing, a therapeutic method based on the wanderings of the desiring vagrant mind—that this becomes clear. But through the attempt to understand something utterly ordinary: Freud found himself simply wanting to know what it meant to be a child, and the child of one's parents, at the particular time when one was growing up. When Freud wrote many years later in his *Autobiographical Study* that in these years he "did little scientific work and published almost nothing. I was occupied in finding my way in my new profession and in securing material subsistence for myself and my rapidly growing family,"[4] he is doing something that he has taught us to understand: he is telling a banal and uninteresting story to conceal a crisis. And we notice, hidden for everyone to see, the stock phrase in this all-too-familiar myth of the struggling young professional man, the sentence, "I was occupied in finding my way in my new profession." He was indeed finding his way, but in what was a completely new profession that he was inventing, and so would literally be his.

So once again, perhaps, we should start with the facts. Partly because these years—between 1887, the year after he married, when he met Wilhelm Fliess, and the publication of *Interpreting Dreams* in 1900—were the most tumultuous years of Freud's life, a protracted crisis in which he had his family, and effectively invented psychoanalysis by inventing a new kind of patient, and a new kind of doctor to treat this patient. And partly because, as Freud warned us in his misgivings about biography and biographers, after the facts there are only what Freud called the "inventions" and "speculations" of biographers (and even some of the facts, as he also acknowledged, could be contested). The biographer, perhaps, was one of those people of "unrestrained imagination" that Jones noted Freud's ambivalence about. Freud, of course, was to write several wildly speculative biographical studies himself.

In this period of Freud's life—as in any period in anyone's life—the discrepancy between the documented and the undocumented life is striking, and can only be imagined. And psychoanalysis, we must remember, in its beginnings was to treat the spoken life, not the documented life; it was originally what people themselves wanted to say, and were able to say about their lives that interested Freud; useful truth was a consequence of dialogue (later, of course, he would "apply" psychoanalysis to larger cultural issues). This, of course, made biography—and in a sense the case history—the enemy of the initial Freudian revolution in truth-telling. So from Freud's correspondence alone during this period, for example, we would assume that Freud, as he says in his *Autobiographical Study*, lived a familial and professional life largely unimpinged upon by political reality. We know much of what Freud wrote during this time, the scientific papers and the correspondence; and we know the history of the times, from historians and from contemporary accounts; but we know very little from Freud himself—very little, that is, in Freud's words—about living in Vienna at the time, a city that by all accounts was at once extraordinarily vibrant and progressive, and degenerately conservative. Freud was always wary of people talking on other people's behalf. So we should note in this crucially transformative period of Freud's life—as, in fact, in most periods of his life—Freud's lack of at least reported interest in his environment. Freud, as Peter Gay put it, "kept aloof from the modern poets and painters and cafe philosophers, and pursued his researches in the austere isolation of his consulting room."[5] When it comes to Freud's Vienna—the now infamous fin de siècle Vienna—Freud's biographers flounder, becoming sketchy and impressionistic, or making lists—a "city of contradictions," a "many-sided society," a "decaying empire," the home of "widespread antisemitism" and the beginnings of Zionism, socialism, and feminism and so on.[6] So the biographer of Freud—at least from Freud's point of view— should, perhaps, stick to the facts, and to Freud's own words; but not always resist what Jones calls, in an odd phrase, "unchecked imagination," especially perhaps in these years of Freud's emerging checked and unchecked imagination.

We must start with the births and the deaths, which give us a clue, at least, about Freud's largely private internal drama (and we should note in passing that in the chronology Ernest Jones provides at the beginning of his authorized biography of Freud the births of his children are not included). In these years the Freuds have six children in quick succession: Mathilde was born in 1887, Martin in 1889, Oliver in 1891, Ernst in 1892, Sophie in 1893, and Anna in 1895. During this time Freud has a growing private practice, writes a number of significant scientific papers, translates a book by Bernheim on hypnotism and suggestion whom he visits in Nancy in 1889, corresponds and meets with Fliess (they call their meetings "congresses"), and begins his self-analysis. But in the background and the foreground are six children born in eight years, and all that that might entail. In the official documented life these are years of extraordinary writings and discoveries; in the undocumented life Freud had a young wife and six children under eight. This, I think, even though, as I say, it can only be imagined—there are glimpses of the children in Freud's correspondence with Fliess, Martin is poetic, Mathilde loves Greek mythology, "Annerl produced her first tooth today," and so on[7]—is the really significant "event" in Freud's life at this time. The return to family life that is the new family. And the recognition of a newfound terror, a newly discovered ambivalence that links one to one's own parents; "Much joy could be had from the little ones," Freud writes to Fliess, "if there were not also so much fright."[8] There is nothing more evocative nor formative in a parent's life than the ages, and the vulnerabilities, of his or her children.

And little is more evocative and formative in everyone's life than the deaths they encounter. In 1896 Freud's father, Jacob, died at the age of eighty-two. Freud would write four years later in *Interpreting Dreams*, in the kind of grand generalization that he was always prone to, and always suspicious of, that "the most important event, the most poignant loss, of a man's life" was his father's death.[9] This may have been a way of registering the profound effect his father's death had on him. He wrote more pointedly to Fliess, at the time, "By the time he died, his

life had long been over, but in my inner self the whole past has
been reawakened by this event. I now feel quite uprooted."[10]
We may wonder what Freud means that his father's life had
long been over (for Freud, or for his father? What is a lived life
like when it is supposedly over?); and we should note how extreme, how unchecked, how unscientific Freud is in this correspondence with Fliess: his "whole past" has been reawakened. But then we must remember that through the trauma of
these years it is precisely the traumatized self—the traumatized
self as the normal, modern self, so to speak—that Freud is beginning to come to terms with. And we must remember that
science was to be the modern cure for trauma, that would itself
become traumatic for Freud. Science, after all, may explain (and
therefore justify) death—not to mention sexuality—but it can't,
as Freud was in the process of realizing, cure us of their existence, or of our feelings about them. Amid the births of his
children in these years there was a catalogue of deaths, that
culminated in the death of his father. A colleague and friend
from his years in Brücke's laboratory, Joseph Paneth, died in
1890; Ernst Fleischl von Marxow, another good friend from his
university years, died in 1892 after years of drug-fueled mental
and physical collapse; in 1892 Brücke died, and in 1893 Charcot
died. And by the 1890s Freud had broken irrevocably with
Breuer. It is, perhaps, unsurprising that in these years Freud
was beginning to really think about people's connections with
each other, about what they exchanged, and wanted to exchange
and failed to exchange with each other; about, in short, sexuality and development and loss. Though no one other than Freud,
who had six children under eight, and lost a father and, sym-
bolically, three fathers and two siblings, ended up writing *Interpreting Dreams*. And that was the kind of singular fact—the
irreducible idiosyncrasy of a life—that Freud was becoming interested in. The losses he began to suffer—the leaving his family of origin, the loss of his father and of other men, the loss of

his wife to their children—sent a depth charge into his own history, reminding him of earlier losses. And all this precipitated him into a unique self-searching, but in a great tradition, as Freud knew only too well, of self-examination. It was only unique in its modernity, in its quest for the pleasures that could make a modern secular life worth living; the recovery and the transformation, that is to say, of the bodily pleasures of childhood.

Everyone was a child and had parents, everyone lost people they loved and admired, and many people had children; but each person's life was their own in a way that was difficult to describe, at least in the language of science. Freud was beginning to think of processes of transformation, of change for human beings as a kind of work (he would soon be writing about dream-work, and later about death-work). But not merely dutiful, or "normative," work, but imaginative and visionary work. There was a biological life cycle that happened in spite of us, and provided us with "natural" limits; and there was the question of what, if anything, we could do, about changing ourselves, selves that were changing whether we wanted them to or not. What Mark Edmundson called the "devoted therapist" in Freud wanted to get people back on track; the Romantic artist, like the Romantic artists before him, valued science, but as itself a figurative and fictive language, a language with its own inevitable limitations. Though science was itself imaginative, indeed sometimes visionary, it tended to describe closed, ineluctable systems; it was to literature you had to go, as Freud knew from his youth, to find the unfinished, the possible, the ecstatic. Through genetics science has shown us how what we have got in common allows us to be different; but genetics, like linguistics, were the sciences that Freud had no access to. He was beginning to wonder how medical treatment—how any kind of intervention—could affect an organism that was described,

in the language of contemporary biology, as an absolutely deterministic system.

Through his work with Charcot and Breuer Freud had
begun to make connections between sexuality, hypnosis, and
hysterical symptoms. Just as he was starting a family himself he
was discovering, we might assume, that childhood was a cumulative trauma in which the child has to make her appetites at
once known and compatible with family life. And that so-called
hysterical patients were the casualties of this process. If he found
himself beginning to link sexuality with a capacity for absorp-
tion, voracious and intent at once—sexuality as somehow spellbinding in the way children are spellbound by their parents—he
was also beginning to describe it as a kind of primordial fear.
Because sexuality begins as incestuous desire for the parents—
as Freud was discovering what he took to be his own and everyone else's Oedipus complex in his self-analysis—it terrorizes
us; and because our primary relation to reality is erotic (i.e., to
the desired parents) whenever we lose ourselves—whatever allows us to forget ourselves—is akin to a sexual act. In these years
we can see a lot of these things dovetailing in Freud's mind, a
lot of things catching up with him. It is as though it begins to
dawn on Freud, partly through studying the complex physiology of appetite, that there is no desire without acculturation;
that for human beings prelinguistic appetites are formed and
reformed and deformed in language. But this Freudian child
developing into language is driven by desire—that through acculturation is called love—and the loss of love, and the fear of
loss of love that loving entails.

As a boy, and as a young man, Freud, as we have seen, was
fascinated by archaeology, by literature, and slowly but surely by
contemporary neurology; history and cultural evolution, what
people had been and what they wanted to be, were his defining
passions. From the panorama of history and the hidden systems

of organic life he was closing in on the individual lives of his contemporaries; and closing in on himself. It is an enclosed life, a life largely hidden—revealed, as I say, in writing and the recorded routines of work and family life—that we see Freud living in this period between his marriage to Martha in 1886 and his publication of *Interpreting Dreams* in 1900. In 1896, after the birth of their last child, Anna, Martha's sister Minna Bernays will come and live with the Freuds as much needed help in bringing up the children, and as company for Freud whose work interested her (Martha, according to the analyst René Laforgue, who knew her, thought Freud's work was "a form of pornography").[11] "My poor Martha," Freud remarked in 1896, "has a tormented life."[12] Freud's refuge from this household of women and children was Wilhelm Fliess, with whom he discussed women and children. The conservative Breuer is displaced in Freud's affections by the more wayward Fliess; a man who believes, to Freud's considerable relief, in the innate bisexuality of human beings.

What absorbed Freud in these years, what he found himself spending more and more time doing as a young professional—at least, from the biographer's point of view—was talking with admired men about disturbed women (and all the biographer can do is reiterate that during the years from 1886 to 1900, Freud had six children in eight years). What these particular medical men wanted to know was what the women were suffering from; and, based on this knowledge, how they might be able to help them. Of course, they had male patients, but women were the focus (*Studies on Hysteria* were all female case studies). So there is a real sense in which psychoanalysis was a science—or an artifact—born of the love between men. It began, that is to say, as a conversation between men about women's bodies (and what will change psychoanalysis is the arrival of women psychoanalysts interested in children as well as sexuality). What these men had in common was an ambitious interest in the treatment of certain kinds of disturbed women (as though their question was, what can you do with the women who disturb you?). So it is important to note at the outset that Freud would insist to the next significant man in his life after Breuer, the idiosyncratic Wilhelm Fliess, that he did not share what he called Fliess's "contempt for friendship between men, probably because I am to a high degree party to it. In my life, as you know, woman has never replaced the comrade, the friend."[13] Though this was written when the relationship was faltering, we should notice here Freud's assumption that the woman should replace the male friend (as though Freud thought there was something odd about himself), and Freud's contempt for Fliess's supposed contempt for friendship between men (despite his commitment to bisexuality). It was, it seems, his relationship with Fliess between 1887 and 1902—conducted mostly through correspondence punctuated by occasional meetings—that carried Freud through this most tumultuous period of his life, and particularly of his marriage. Years in which Freud would become extremely interested in himself and become temporarily— in his correspondence with Fliess and in *Interpreting Dreams*— his own biographer; in which it began to dawn on him that he could only know himself through the knowing of others, that self-knowledge was collaborative and provisional; and in which it would also begin to dawn on him what an odd kind of knowledge self-knowledge was, strangely compelling and often strikingly ineffectual. And in this period of exceptionally hard work he would discover a new kind of work called dream-work; a kind of work that was at once inspired, astoundingly inventive, and thoughtful, and that required neither effort nor training; and that people did in their sleep. It was to be Freud's most startling and radical notion.

This "heroic period" of Freud's life were years, in Masud Khan's words, "of acute stress, anguish, anxiety, distress, discouragement and exultation of unmatchable discoveries. . . . sustained for Freud by his relation to Fliess."[14] We should imagine Freud in these years living an extremely routinized, moderately successful professional life of private practice in Vienna, as a doctor of neuropathy, with a large young family, in a state of great turmoil, that he had to write himself out of, or through. He had lost a father, and become a father himself; he had established a niche in the medical world, without really wanting to be a doctor; and he had inherited a language—a set of scientific descriptions, a vocabulary—that was not sufficient for what he had to say. Out of the safe familiarity of bourgeois Jewish family life Freud would make his last attempt at a scientifically reputable neurophysiological account of what he called, in the instrumental language of science, "the psychic apparatus," entitled appropriately, though not by Freud but by his editors, the "Project for a Scientific Psychology" (it was begun, they tell us, on a train after a meeting with Fliess). And through the inevitable failure of this project—inevitable because of the limits of the science that was available to him, and because of his suspicions about the language of science—Freud broke through to the more literary, the more psychological account of *Interpreting Dreams*, in which the so-called psychic apparatus began to sound more like a poet than a machine. In which the making of tropes replaced the binding and discharge of stimulation, and dreams were described as sophisticated experiences rather than neuronal reflexes, as Freud begins to release the language of literature into the language of science, to make the hybrid language of psychoanalysis (to compare any page of the "Project for a Scientific Psychology" with a page of *Interpreting Dreams* is to see what C. P. Snow meant by the two cultures of the arts and the sciences). It is not accidental that in this period Freud was so taken with the mixture of wackiness and hard science that was Wilhelm Fliess. Nor is it surprising that, as a Jew in an often hostile environment—and as a young man going through what we would learn to call, largely through his work, an iden-

tity crisis—he would be increasingly suspicious of the authorities, preferring people of doubtful authority to the legitimate
and the entitled, preferring the interesting thing to the (supposedly) real thing. In this formative period of his life Freud
moves from wondering who to believe in, to wondering about
the origins and the function of the individual's predisposition
to believe.

Brücke and Breuer, in their very different ways, had been
respectable professional men, beyond reproach in their given
scientific disciplines. Beginning with Charcot—not to mention the "hysterical" and so-called mentally ill patients that he
treated—Freud was increasingly drawn to the more eccentric
less reputable types, those who were not quite so easily assimilated by the official culture; those who created suspicion and
unease; the charismatic and the bizarre; the people who may
or may not be frauds or charlatans. Jews, after all, were inau-
thentic Austrians and Germans. Fliess, another Jew, believed in
male and female periods—the "male cycle" was, according to
him, twenty-three days—and in what he called "the nasal reflex
neurosis," based on the supposed similarity between nasal and
genital tissue. He was regarded by many of his contemporaries
as a fascinating man and doctor. But, as Louis Breger writes,
"In addition to his work as a doctor, he put forth wide-ranging
biological theories; some physicians and scientists saw these
as great discoveries while others viewed them as quackery."[15]
Freud and his followers would soon be described in exactly
this way, encouraged to feel fraudulent while investigating the
provenance and purpose of all the horrifyingly severe *internal*
judgments that modern people were prone to (to feel a fraud is
to have already consented to the standards you are being judged
by). Freud, in other words, was beginning to find his level ("You
have taught me," Freud wrote in gratitude to Fliess in 1896,
"that a bit of truth lurks behind every popular lunacy").[16] Just
as he would be drawn to the unofficial thinking and feeling of

the unconscious, and the unofficial as opposed to the official development of the modern individual, Freud gravitated towards Fliess as a soul mate. And as always between soul mates, it took time for the very real differences between them to become apparent. And by the time they were, Freud had found his own way and no longer needed Fliess.

Of course, all the proliferating sciences of the nineteenth century were largely male pursuits; and in the medical sciences, authority was always in question, since medical knowledge was only believable and effective when it was curative. But what distinguished the psychoanalysis that Freud was inventing in these years was that it was a science of human relationships, an account of human development and purpose that made sexuality and the relations between the sexes the cause, the explanation (and therefore the justification) of all human endeavor ("neurasthenia can in fact only be a sexual neurosis," Freud wrote to Fliess in 1893).[17] Exchange between people was at once the source and the subject; and exchange, Freud had begun to think, was essentially sexual in origin, and by analogy. Once Freud discovered, through analysing his own dreams, his "single idea" everything fell into place: "A single idea of general value dawned on me," he wrote to Fliess. "I have found in my own case too, the phenomena of being in love with my mother and jealous of my father, and I now consider it a universal event in early childhood."[18] This single idea—so ordinary and obvious until Freud elaborated it in his own way—contained, as we shall see, many ideas (it could explain rivalry, ambition, jealousy, envy, pride, authority, religion, communism, scarcity, abjection, success, failure, mourning, and murder, among other things). Though it took some time for Freud to realize this, once he had made sexuality and the child's relations with the parents the heart of the matter the concept of cure, the nature of belief, and the status of authority (scientific, or otherwise) were all put into question. In retrospect we can see that Freud was opening up, through the treatment of so-called hysterics, the Pandora's box of his culture. He was exposing and redescribing, exposing by redescribing, virtually everything that mattered most to the culture he lived in.

For Freud, as we have seen—and working with so-called hysterics had been a kind of initiation rite—his work was increasingly collaborative, and about the struggle for collaboration. The hysteric's symptoms were her self-cure for failures of collaboration with, and between, the parents (they were involved in the wrong kinds of exchange within the family). The doctor was still the one in the know, but he depended on the patient's words; not unlike the parent loving and desiring the child's words as he begins to speak, the new kind of doctor Freud was inventing was as much a facilitator as an informer, as much of a recipient as an instructor; like and unlike a parental figure. And Fliess was essentially a recipient and a facilitator for Freud in these years; unwittingly, like a psychoanalyst, he allowed Freud to have his own thoughts, barely informing him about anything much (Freud only took on Fliess's ideas about bisexuality, but they were mostly not original, and Freud had thought about bisexuality before he met Fliess). Freud in other words was becoming interested in what might be called the erotics of collaboration—in what people could and couldn't do together; with each other, and with themselves. In his relationship with Fliess Freud both theorized and enacted the erotic complications of collaboration. The great discoveries of these years were a growing sense of the power and provenance of fantasy, a method for interpreting dreams, and an understanding of the Oedipus complex which linked together became a story about sexuality and an unconscious mind, a part of the mind that thought differently. Then the lesser discovery of these years— one that was integral to Freud's pressing preoccupation about the nature of love—was that Fliess was not quite the man Freud had thought he was. And that Martha, of course, as a mother of six children was different from the girl who had been his fiancée for all those years. But the deaths and births and catastrophic disillusionments of these years did not disillusion Freud; rather, they made him interested in disillusionment. And in disillusionment not as a cynicism, or a nihilism—or even a pessimism, at least at first—but as the precondition for satisfaction.

I

So it is not incidental that in his correspondence with Fliess Freud can sound like someone in love. In over three hundred letters that they wrote to each other, having met first in 1887, Freud is often solicitous and effusive. "I still do not know how I won you," Freud writes in 1888 after Fliess has attended one of his lectures in the early years of their friendship, "the bit of speculative anatomy of the brain [the subject of Freud's lecture] cannot have impressed your rigorous judgement for long,"[19] Freud acknowledging, as it were, that scientific enlightenment may not be the key to love. Freud writes of looking forward to their "congresses" as to "the slaking of hunger and thirst."[20] In 1893 he writes, "You altogether ruin my critical faculties, and I really believe you in everything;"[21] "You are the only other, the alter" he writes the following year.[22] When Freud had anxieties about his heart in 1894 it was Fliess, whom he called his "magical healer," that he told and not Martha. When the Freuds stopped having sex, possibly for contraceptive reasons, it was Fliess whom Freud told, and who knew the reasons ("We are now living in abstinence; and you know the reasons for this as well").[23] In 1895 the sight of Fliess's handwriting in a letter helped Freud "forget much loneliness and privation."[24] By 1893 Freud was addressing Fliess as "beloved friend." Freud's passion for Fliess was the medium, in both senses, for his own development.

Between the older men that Freud admired and courted and

the younger men (and few women) who would soon admire and court him, there was then the unusual Wilhelm Fliess, just two years younger than Freud, who would be the bridge, as it were, between the young Freud and the first great psychoanalyst he was to become. And it is in his writing—above all in his correspondence with Fliess and *Interpreting Dreams*, in which there are so few references to politics, to economics, to the city, to signs of the times—that we can read the sea change that happens between the so-called "Project for a Scientific Psychology" (written in 1895) and the new kind of psychology that was *Interpreting Dreams*, Freud's revolutionary book written, appropriately, at the very end of the century. In 1891 the Freud family moved to the more spacious Berggasse 19 where the Freuds were to live for the next forty-seven years; an address that would become legendary in what became the history of psychoanalysis; as the family home, as his consulting room with the famous couch and the equally famous collection of antiquities. For Freud it was the house on which he hoped there would one day be a plaque in commemoration. "Do you suppose," he wrote to Fliess, "that someday one will read on a marble tablet on this house: Here, on July 24, 1895, / The secret of the dream / revealed itself to Dr. Sigm. Freud."[25] It is phrased as something akin to a revelation (or a visitation), "the dream revealed itself," Freud chosen for the revelation. And it is a mark of Freud's extraordinary and exhilarating ambition that it would be *the* secret of the dream, not one among many.

In this decisive period, a period of withdrawn self-absorption —almost like a period of illness, or incubation—amid the clamor of family life and a demanding clinical schedule, Freud will move in his theory from a biological determinism, to a questioning of the nature of this biological determinism and what it may have excluded, or underestimated—acculturation, and the idea of choice and agency (the psychoanalyst believes, by definition, that he and the patient can intervene in an otherwise deterministic system); from a picture of the individual as victim, as immigrant, as supplicant to the individual as also self-fashioning, entitled, and ingenious in his desiring. A sense of the individual's powerful and significant agency—albeit unconscious—is being restored as Freud discovers and recovers his own powers of imaginative speculation. From having believed that neuroses were caused by adults sexually abusing children, he will begin to describe, in his famous modification of the so-called seduction theory, that children also desire adults, and therefore adults' sexual attention, but in fantasy (not in reality); that the cause of neurosis in adults is the albeit conflicted but actively desirous fantasizing of the child about her parents, in which the child assumes a right to her own gratification, and imperiously attempts to organize a world that will satisfy her (Freud never denied that unacceptable things were done to children, he just added that children also want to do unacceptable things). As well as there being a cause of neurosis Freud will begin to refer to a "choice of neurosis." And in *Interpreting Dreams* Freud will describe the dreamer as an unconsciously active maker, as an artist using the history of his own past desiring to secure future satisfactions. And doing this by contriving those most sophisticated artifacts, dreams; Freud following on from Nietzsche's suggestion that every person is an artist in their dreams. The dreamer tells himself secrets at night about what he wants (like an informer, spying on his past; and particularly on the unmet needs of his past). And far from describing the modern individual as a divided self he will describe him as wildly and unpredictably and unknowably and unknowingly various in his desires, irresolvably conflicted, but entirely of a piece (it being essentially defensive to divide oneself).

But above all Freud will see sexuality as both the way the individual, in the Darwinian sense, survives and reproduces, but also—at the same time—as the way the individual makes and repeats his own history; because in Freud's view one's history is encoded in one's sexual desire. The hysterics symptoms were her sexual desire Freud remarked in the *Studies on Hysteria;* and Freud could say this because he realized that the hysteric in describing her symptoms was telling him a disguised story of her life. After all, what could a history of one's life be, but a history of one's needs and wants, and the inevitable conflicts around them? To be a sexual person is to be historically minded, whether one is aware of this, or not. For human animals our needs always involve the history of our needs. The making conscious Freud was beginning to propose as the essential therapy was an attempt to remind the patient of her desire. Freud's youthful, idealistic assumption being that knowledge of one's desire would make it less persecutory. Freud, we can see now, was trying to imagine, in the early years of psychoanalysis, what it would be for a modern person to be—and it is, of course appropriate that a Jew might have proposed this—neither a guest nor a host, neither a master nor a slave, neither a victor nor a victim in relation to his own desire; as well, of course, as being all those things. So before the external dramas of establishing what would become the psychoanalytic movement there had to be the internal dramas of what Freud was becoming by beginning to establish what psychoanalysis might be. Not something that came from nowhere—like everything else Freud's work comes out of a confluence of traditions—but something that also proposed a new place, an "other scene" from where things come, called the unconscious. The matrix of nature and the bit of nature we call culture.

II

No one would read the unpublished "Project for a Scientific Psychology" now unless they were interested in it as part of the history of neurophysiology, or the history of its author. In the years in which Freud was writing it, his editors tell us, "the dominant idea in Freud's mind was to make physiological changes and the physically measureable the basis of all psychological discussion; in other words his aim was the strict application of ideas derived from Helmholtz and Brücke."[26] It is, they go on to tell us, a coherent attempt to describe the functioning of the psychical apparatus as that of a system of neurones and to conceive of "all the processes concerned as in the last resort quantitative."[27] In this text which was the pretext for *Interpreting Dreams*, we can see Freud, in brief, trying to give quasi-mathematical accounts of the human organism's transformations of energy, as a way of explaining symptoms of so-called mental illness. The human organism is described as a machine for managing excitement; to regulate the internal stimuli of need, which is instinct driven, as it meets the stimuli of the external world, through "discharge" and what is called the "binding" of energy. Freud distinguishes between free energy and bound energy; the psychic apparatus is there to bind the free energy that is always threatening to overwhelm the organism. It is the ego's job to bind this energy, and thinking and speech are deemed to be the essential forms of bound energy (the picture is of something powerful and inchoate and potentially overwhelming seeking form and containment). Despite the recondite specialist language, in which we see Freud competently speaking the language of the tribe he aspires to be a distinguished member of—"it is reasonable to suppose that in the act of thinking a small stream of motor innervation passes from psi—but only, of course, if during that act a motor or a key neurone is innervated,"[28] and so on—it is a simple picture of the organism as persecuted, as perpetually under threat from its own needs and from a hostile or resistant external world; an organism always about to be destroyed by the instincts and the environment that sustain it. It is a peculiarly modern picture of a life, and one that might have its attractions for an immigrant

Jew—though, clearly, not only for an immigrant Jew—trying to make his way in the often antisemitic ethos of the Viennese medical profession. It is, for example, a view redescribed in the language of economics and class by another Jew, Karl Marx.

Of course Freud engages in no such special pleading. But under the aegis of the universalizing language of science—which apparently frees everyone to be just a human being of no particular place or class or time—Freud does something very interesting with the picture. He reframes it as a story about infancy, and about human nature; it is the nature of human beings—dependent for far longer than any other mammal—to be fundamentally and perpetually infantile, whatever else they are. He suggests that the fundamental picture of a human being is as a screaming baby, screaming babies being something that Freud would have been more than familiar with at this time. So there is one section of the Project that seems particularly pertinent for the biographer, about, as it were, the beginning of the story of a life. When the child is hungry, Freud writes:

> Experience shows that the first path to be followed is that leading to internal change (e.g., emotional expression, scream-ing, or vascular innervation). But . . . no discharge of this kind can bring about any relief of tension, because endoge-nous stimuli continue to be received in spite of it . . . Here the removal of a stimulus can be effected only by an inter-vention which will temporarily stop the release of quantity in the interior of the body, and an intervention of this kind requires an alteration of the external world (e.g., the supply of nourishment, or the proximity of the sexual object) and this, as a "specific action" can be brought about only in par-ticular ways. At early stages the human organism is incapable of achieving this specific action. It is brought about by extra-neous help, when the attention of an experienced person has been drawn to the child's condition by a discharge taking place along the path of internal change (e.g., by the child's scream-

ing). The path of discharge thus acquires an extremely important secondary function—viz. of bringing about an understanding with other people; and the original helplessness of
human beings is thus the primal source of all moral motives.
When the extraneous helper has carried out the specific action in the external world on behalf of the helpless subject,
the latter is in a position, by means of reflex contrivances,
immediately to perform what is necessary in the interior of
his body in order to remove the endogenous stimuli. This
total event then constitutes an "experience of satisfaction,"
which has the most momentous consequences in the func-
tional development of the individual.[29]

In these two paragraphs Freud provides one of the essential
building blocks of psychoanalysis; and in these two paragraphs
we can see the overlap, perhaps unsurprisingly, of lived experience (the family) and the language of science (of Freud and
Fliess) combining to make something unusually suggestive and
far-reaching (among other things a story about the origins of
morality). Freud at home in these years would have done virtually nothing but observe (and possibly participate in) the scene
described here. And in the middle of this scene, presumably,
there would be, for Freud, the question of his own satisfaction
(and survival) amid all the need and mothering going on. And
it would not be excessive to say that here Freud announces the
entire psychoanalytic project; the attempt to give an account of
the connection between survival and the fate of satisfaction in
a person's life. And the psychoanalytic question: How does the
individual survive his appetite, which is the source of his survival, Freud linking here, in the psychoanalytic way, hunger and
sexuality, infancy and adulthood? In this picture it is clear that
life can only be lived in relation (the child would die of hunger
without his need being recognized and met); that dependence
is the precondition for survival and satisfaction (so independence becomes a variant of dependence, not a superseding of

it). Freud will develop a therapy, psychoanalysis, that reiterates the initial and initiating couple of mother and child. The scene described here will be the blueprint for the psychoanalytic setting in which needs are articulated, as far as is possible, but are met only with words, all in the service of making the patient's appetite viable (ultimately, outside the consulting room). The dream, in Freud's account, will be the place, the activity, in which the individual formulates his (largely unconscious) need in the internal world. The dream, in a sense, is the homework of desire: the preparation: the always wishful foretaste.

The child and his mother; the dreamer and his dream; the patient and his psychoanalyst. Freud's psychoanalytic story begins as a story about a couple; with the idea that appetite (and desire) only become viable through representation, recognition, and care. And evolves into a story about the meaning, structure, and function of dreams. In Freud's analysis of his own dreams the father begins to join in, joins the mother and child to make the essential triangle; and to fully constitute, as we shall see, the child's desire. In the psychoanalytic treatment that Freud is inventing now, which takes place again in a couple (excluding third parties), not in a threesome—though the world outside the consulting room is an always pressing third party— it will be the viability of appetite that will be at stake; that appetite, ultimately for life, without which life is not worth living (Freud's question from here on in is: what are the sustaining satisfactions for the modern individual?). The dream, in Freud's account, will be no more and no less than a bulletin from the source of the individual's life. News from the past for the future. Freud, in his self-analysis, was beginning to remember bits and pieces of (or from) his own past; and the news is addressed, at first, to Fliess.

5

———◆•◆•◆———

Psychoanalysis Comes Out

The most violent revolutions in an individual's
beliefs leave most of his old order standing.
—William James, *Pragmatism*

FREUD BEGINS TO TELL HIS STORY about psychoanalysis—a
story, as we have seen, that begins to crystallize in the 1880s—
by describing the child's ambition for survival as a quest for
pleasure. And pleasure involved the regulation of feelings that
always threatened to overwhelm. Freud's psychology was about
the alien and the excessive; about appetite described as a foreign
body, invasive and ineluctable. The (fictional) ego in Freud's
emerging story—a term not invented by Freud, but popular-
ized by him, that the new discipline of psychology had im-
ported from philosophy—was an immigrant; the body's often
unwelcome guest. In inventing psychoanalysis Freud was beginning to give an account of the fate of the unassimilable in

his patients' lives. And more generally, he was beginning to account for—something starkly pertinent for the Jews of Freud's generation—what one makes of what one is forced by.

What does the child want, and how does he do his wanting were now Freud's abiding preoccupations as he himself was beginning to discover what he wanted from and for psychoanalysis, and the form his ambition should take. It was dawning on Freud that whatever story we are telling, we are always also telling the story of our own wanting. So at any moment in Freud's life we can ask, encouraged and legitimated by his own work, what is Freud wanting from psychoanalysis? What is the pleasure he seeks? What is he doing it for and what is it doing for him? What about himself is he seeking to sustain and enjoy, and what would he prefer to ignore? Though, of course, as Freud insists, the answers to these questions are largely speculative in his absence.

From what he had gleaned in his self-analysis Freud was beginning to realize—in the aftermath of the literature of Romanticism, reformulated in the language of his contemporary sciences—what it might mean that the story of a life was the (reworked) story of a childhood. "Child psychology," he wrote in *Interpreting Dreams*, "is destined to perform the same useful services for adult psychology that the investigation of the structure or development of the lower animals has performed for research into the structure of the higher classes of animals."[1] The adult is what the child, in this analogy, evolves into, for Freud the evolutionary biologist. But as a father Freud had noticed something equally profound—indeed, the whole history of psychoanalysis came out of this simple observation; children only survived, because someone looked after them; someone was there helping them to bear their feelings; and something was driving them to be looked after, to have their needs sufficiently attended to. The analyst, Freud realized, was—albeit belatedly—doing something akin to parenting (or rather, something that would be experienced by the patient as reminiscent of parenting); in the psychoanalytic setting Freud unconsciously re-created the early situation of infant care in which a parent attentively, and in the fullest sense, listens to his or her child. The infant is born a desiring creature; but to be viable, to be promising, to be hopeful as a desiring creature his desires, and later his words, have to be addressed to another person who can recognize them. And for this to happen the excitement of desire—what Freud called in the "Project for a Scientific Psychology" the "stimuli"—had to be "bound," formed, contained. At first a cry is the form the infant's desire takes, and then, gradually, words. The adult's give form, through their responses, to the pleas of the child. The excitement of desiring was a communication, and only worked insofar as it was a communication; and a communication, Freud was beginning to realize, was as good as its listener—as good as its listener can make it—just as a joke is as good as its audience. What Freud was increasingly interested in was how instinctual desire made itself known, and how the modern human animal made itself known, to itself and others, through its desire. It was the meaning of what a person couldn't help but do that Freud wanted to make sense of, so vivid in childhood, and in sexuality; and in the dreams and slips and symptoms of adults that were, he now believed, the recurring expression of childhood sexuality. So-called symptoms were ways of keeping sexuality alive and in circulation (the patient's symptoms are his sexual life, as Freud famously remarked); ways of living our desire in a modern world. Our helplessness, within a family, is where we start from: and above all, we are helplessly desiring creatures. As a Darwinian the young Freud believed that we have nothing to show for ourselves but our means of survival. By 1920—after the First World War and the death of his favourite daughter, Sophie—Freud would speculate in *Beyond the Pleasure Principle* that we are also driven by that contradiction in terms—an instinct for death.

The child depended on the mother to sufficiently recognize and meet his need; the psychoanalytic patient depended on the analyst to help her articulate her need. It was these correspondences, the fit and the misfit—between instinctual desire and its objects, between need and language, between the individual and his environment—that had now become, we can see in retrospect, Freud's abiding preoccupations. These are, of course, things that parents of young children, like Freud himself, are thinking about. Freud was simply developing a new, more modern language for these common concerns. And like the developing child he described he too was finding the forms of language he needed for what he had to say, both as a clinician and as a writer. The psychoanalyst he was inventing was a doctor who only spoke, and wrote; who had to find the right words, the right kind of conversation, for his patients.

It was, as we can see now, ultimately his relationship with Fliess—which mostly took the form of a correspondence—and his interest in his own dreams that changed Freud from being an aspiring neuroanatomist into a pioneering psychoanalyst with a famous name. Work that had begun as collaborative experimental science in a laboratory had finally come down, via the treatment of hysterical patients, to a man in his home, dreaming and writing about his dreams. The basic material of his newfound work was the common currency of dreams and words, our second nature. Speaking and dreaming, the most ordinary things we do, requiring no specialist training, no formal education. Everyone has a past, and virtually everyone speaks and dreams. His subject was the ordinary activity of appetite, and its imaginative transformations. With his consulting room in the house in which he lived, his domestic life and his professional life combined at Berggasse 19, Freud began his (therapeutic) enquiry into the relationship between the public and the private life of the people he saw. To invent psychoanalysis Freud needed, above all, at this crucial period of his life, to be able to sleep, to talk, and to write. He discovered psychoanalysis in his sleep.

It is when Freud starts thinking, in his early forties, about dreams—and about what he will call in *Interpreting Dreams* "dream-work"—that he becomes a psychoanalyst. His voluminous book is about the dream in its many aspects beginning, appropriately, with the history of dream interpretation, because the psychoanalyst is essentially a historian. Sex was mostly interesting to Freud because of what it revealed about the individual's development. The dream as Freud's object of desire; the dream described by Freud as the individual's eccentric way of thinking about—of formulating in disguised form—his objects of desire; the dream as akin to an enigmatic work of art; and above all the dream as at once private and public. No one witnesses or experiences it other than the dreamer, but it can only be dreamt and reported in the recognizable and shared language of images and words. The language of dreams, Freud realized, was a language that no one had ever been taught, but one that everyone had learned and could use; and yet, at the same time, it seemed to be a language that was rarely understood. It was literally spellbinding for the dreamer in his dream, but it was all too easily forgotten. (The dream often fades on waking without our knowing what happens to it.) Why would we use a language that we were so keen to forget? And Freud's answer was that dreaming was the language of forbidden (oedipal, childhood) desire; and that the forbidden was too disturbing because it was too alluring.

As a language, Freud realized—and the history of dream interpretation that he recounted in the opening chapters of *Interpreting Dreams* showed—dreams must be a communication, but to whom and about what? Freud was to describe the dream as addressed to the dreamer—the dream was a way the dreamer told himself secrets at night about his desire; but that in order for the messages to reach the dreamer the dream, in the first instance needed to be addressed, Freud now proposed, to a psychoanalyst who had a method for understanding the dream, and a good idea of what it was about. *Interpreting Dreams* was Freud's primer of psychoanalysis; an account of how he thought the mind worked, and of how psychoanalysis worked by interpreting the patient's free associations to the elements of his dream. So what Freud called the "latent content" of the dream— the infantile wishes it encoded—were revealed through the "manifest content" of the dream, the words in which the dreamer describes his dream. Whether Freud had discovered the meaning of dreams in his book, or simply a method through which dreams could reveal their unpredictable meanings, was always unclear. The question was whether the psychoanalyst knew what was in the unconscious, or whether what was a contradiction in terms would become a major controversy both within and outside the psychoanalytic movement. It was a version of the question, Is the psychoanalyst the person who knows what words refer to? Once Freud had discovered what he called the unconscious it was never clear how unconscious the unconscious would be allowed to be (at least by the owners of psychoanalysis). What would it be to be an expert or a specialist of the unconscious? And yet the sentences of Freud's psychoanalysis— that for Freud were always only speculative—were all about how the unconscious worked, as a quite foreign way of thinking; and how it worked, essentially, in relation to desired others. Why otherwise would the unconscious, as Freud's follower Lacan later formulated it, be structured like a language? Freud was discovering that thinking was a form of conversation, but that we also think differently from the way we think we think. And we want differently from the way we want to want.

Between 1898, when Freud began working on what would become *Interpreting Dreams,* and 1905 Freud would do the two essential things for the founding of a movement: he would write and publish founding texts, the seminal texts of psychoanalysis, in which he described unconscious mental functioning—*Interpreting Dreams* (1900), *The Psychopathology of Everyday Life* (1901), *Fragment of an Analysis of a Case of Hysteria, Three Essays on the Theory of Sexuality*, and *Jokes and Their Relation to the Unconscious* (1905). And he would attract a group of interested followers. At first a small group, the now-famous Wednesday Society that began in 1902 with five members, all Jewish doctors—Wilhelm Stekel, Alfred Adler, Max Kahane, and Rudolph Reiter—that would become in 1908 the Vienna Psychoanalytic Society. And in that year the first International Congress of Psychoanalysis would be held in Salzburg, with forty-two analysts attending, mostly from Austria and Switzerland but also from Germany, Hungary, the United States, and England. Freud, that is to say, in these years of escalating interest in his work, was confronted with something that psychoanalysis itself was a way of thinking about: how to make the private and personal public. Freud was transforming the private treatment of psychoanalysis into public writings and lectures. Making it as available as possible for public consideration. And this, of course, was a version of what Freud was describing in the psychobiological development of the individual; every individual struggled to publicize (and to conceal for protection) his private world, struggled to socialise his need, to make himself known in the service of survival and reproduction. The privacy of the dream and of sexuality, the individual's personal history, the impersonal privacy of the psychoanalytic setting and treatment; all this Freud was in the process, in these years, of describing —and slowly but surely popularizing, to a small but growing audience—in what was emerging as a distinctively psychoanalytic language. A language with its own jargon and set of assumptions. Words like id, ego, superego, repression would soon be common currency, so contagious was this new language for the heart and soul and conscience of modern people.

Psychoanalysis, then, was in these early years at the turn of the century, making links with a wider audience—becoming interesting to artists and intellectuals, to feminists and socialists—and was itself about making new links between the private and the public in what were beginning to be called the new mass societies of Europe (psychoanalysis was something that people did in cities). Societies in which more and more people, apparently unmoored from the traditions of previous generations, were experiencing a troubling disparity between their internal world of thought and feeling, and the societies in which they lived; between their family histories and their present cultural (i.e., economic) circumstances; between the stuff of their fantasies and their erotic and political lives. But this making of new links was a form of individual therapy, a branch of the medical profession, not, at least for Freud, a politics by other means. Freud's conscious ambition was the alleviation of the individual's neurotic suffering. He was increasingly interested not in whether his work was of any political significance—it would be some of his later left-wing followers like Wilhelm Reich and Paul Federn who would wonder about this; Freud's followers kept reminding Freud of what he had omitted (or repressed) in his psychoanalytic theorizing—but with the question of whether his often edifying and illuminating descriptions were useful and therapeutically effective. Whether they were true pragmatically, or only speculatively.

There was a split in German and Austrian fin de siècle medical culture between the physicians and the academics, a split which psychoanalysis would attempt to bridge. "A small but prestigious university faculty," the historian of psychoanalysis George Makari writes, "insisted on furthering science, while most medical practitioners did what they could to master often unproven therapies." Commenting on this situation the German physician Rudolph Virchow drily observed, "It is said of the academic physician that he can do nothing, and of the practitioner that he knows nothing."[2] In a contemporary medical profession in which, absurdly, knowledge outstripped clinical competence—in which the more physicians knew about the working of the body the less they felt able to do to alleviate suffering—Freud was wanting a "psychological science" that made a desirable difference to his patient's lives. He didn't want to be the kind of doctor who was supposed to know things that didn't make a difference. He wasn't interested in science for science's sake. Indeed he would make an understanding of what the patient expected to get from the doctor—what she expected the doctor to know—integral to his new form of "psychological treatment." He would describe the obstacles to the treatment as the means of treatment. What he called the "transference" in his *Fragment of an Analysis of a Case of Hysteria* (the "Dora" case)—what the patient transferred on to the doctor as expectation, hope, and fear—Freud would see as an essential clue to the patient's suffering. The patient's expectations of the doctor derived, Freud realized, from earlier expectations, both wished-for and feared, satisfied and frustrated, in their families of origin. If the patient's wanting was to become more realistic, less fixated in the past, these expectations, these assumed blueprints of relationship, needed to be made conscious. Freud's hope, in these years, was that making things conscious extended the individual's realm of choice; where there was compulsion there might be decision, or newfound forms of freedom. In the beginning, psychoanalysis, in other words, was the young Freud's attempt to have some new ideas about authority. Many of Freud's followers would lose this appetite to think differently about authority.

In the case of Dora—which exposes with unwitting honesty, the draws and the drawbacks of Freud's clinical style, and of psychoanalytic treatment itself—we see Freud making unexpected connections between Dora's symptoms and her family history. We see the drama of forbidden wishful expectations as the drama of bourgeois family life. And we see Freud failing in his own account of the treatment, because he had been unable to recognize what Dora expected of him. "What are transferences?" Freud asks in his commentary on the case. "They are new editions or facsimiles of the impulses and phantasies that are aroused and made conscious during the progress of the analysis; but they have this peculiarity, which is characteristic of their species, that they replace some earlier person by the person of the physician."[3] Once again writing and the publishing of books are the analogies that come to mind for Freud, with the word "species" reminding us of Freud's divided duty, his loyalty as ever for both the biological and the literary. Freud is characteristically self-questioning, interested equally in what works, and how it works.

In Freud's view his patients were suffering from a diminished —that is to say, repressed, and therefore distorted—awareness of their real desires. Desires that were out of print, and needed to be back in circulation. The hysteric, the obsessional, the neurotic were failed and failing hedonists; they were compromising their pleasure in the service of their survival. They were trying to recover lost opportunities, missed chances, uncompleted actions. But it was the albeit ancient idea of people as essentially pleasure-seeking animals that was the organizing principle of Freud's theory and practice. Pleasure-seeking was something that the abstracted academics and the pragmatic doctors might share. And lurking here, though it would take Freud and his followers some time to broach it, was the whole issue of the psychoanalyst's pleasure; of what exactly was gratifying about practicing as an analyst.

In this extraordinary burst of writing at the turn of the century Freud emerges as a visionary pragmatist; a doctor with a new effective therapeutic method—not quite a technique and not simply a talent; and not, it turned out, quite as effective as he wished—with one main project: an understanding of the patient's pleasure-seeking, and how it was linked into his survival.

Freud was a medical practitioner with a new story about the possibilities of human pleasure (which would include a story about the hedonism of suffering), and that linked evolutionary biology with psychological science. Freud saw the struggle for survival as a struggle for pleasure. Darwin had told a new and revolutionary story about sexuality as a biological imperative; and Freud, in his own view, was following on from there. What was at stake in the new treatment of psychoanalysis, as Freud began to formulate it at the turn of the century, was whether the patient could recover the pleasures that would make his life seem worth living. And these, essentially, were the pleasures of childhood, and their later variants (Freud, for example, famously suggests in a letter to Fliess that the reason no adult is really satisfied by money is because children don't want money). Freud, in early middle age, with a young family, became preoccupied with growing up as an experience of loss and diminishment; with a sense of the mismatch of childhood and adulthood, of development felt as failure and adulthood as a strange kind of defeatedness, a time, for many modern people, of an increasingly impoverished sense of possibility. It was through his newfound confidence as a father, a writer, and a clinician, that Freud could begin to think about how much confidence could be lost in development.

Modern people, it seemed to Freud, were the only animals that were ambivalent about their own development; they longed to grow up and they hated growing up, and sabotaged it. In other words, we can see Freud now, consciously or unconsciously, wanting to pick up the threads of an abandoned Romanticism, and reworking them in a scientific, predominantly Darwinian context. The child, the dream, development as the narrowing of the mind and the stifling of the heart; society as the enemy of the individual's passion and vision; the suspicion of traditional forms of authority; a new exhilaration about the possibilities of language. These are the themes and the hauntings of European Romanticism, and of Freud's psychoanalysis (Karl Furtmüller described the Vienna Psychoanalytic Society that he joined in 1909 as "a sort of catacomb of romanticism, a small and daring group, persecuted now but bound to conquer the world.")[4] It is not incidental that in these years Freud's writing becomes increasingly less technical and more accessible to the interested reader; its radical implications—soon to be taken up by Freud's early followers Sandor Ferenczi and Wilhelm Reich who Freud would ultimately have to discredit—muffled by its all-too-bourgeois therapeutic ambitions; its accessible clarity barely containing its strange provocations.

If the nineteenth century novel and the biography were the contemporary literary genres—the post-Romantic literary genres—available for the (literate) modern individual of the late nineteenth century to consider his or her pleasures (often called ambitions), to make more public the private struggle to make a life, psychoanalysis would follow on from them. Freud had described in his and Breuer's *Studies on Hysteria* a new use, a therapeutic use, for the telling of life stories; now Freud was beginning to see dreams, jokes, and mistakes as both integral and essential to these life stories. Freud was discovering what, if anything, the new languages of science had to contribute to this project of finding adequate—that is, therapeutic—forms of narrative coherence; a way of telling and contributing to a patient's telling of that person's life story that would disclose a repressed repertoire of possibilities (this was the undeclared, or repressed legacy, of Romanticism that psychoanalysis revitalized). If Freud was wondering what people were talking about when they were talking about their suffering—when they were talking about their symptom-ridden lives—he was also noticing what they needed to omit to make their life stories seem plausible and coherent; and how often, for modern people—at least the modern people who were his patients—talking about their lives was talking about their resistance to—their fear of, their sabotaging of, their horror of—pleasure, and the feeling of aliveness that comes with it. Freud was interested in what happened to whatever, in the patient's experience of himself, couldn't be assimilated, couldn't be easily included in the narrative. Sexuality was an emblem of the unassimilable (Judaism was another such emblem).

Indeed it sometimes seems in Freud's first great psychoanalytic writing at the turn of the century that he is trying to rescue the whole notion of pleasure; as if the modern person's sustaining pleasures—of religion, of rootedness, of family, of sexuality—were radically under threat. Once there was despair about the traditional, the conventional, the familiar pleasures, pleasure might have to be found in despair itself, and the other allied forms of suffering. For many secularized modern people —and most of Freud's personal and professional circles were nonobservant Jews—the suffering of life had become futile. If suffering didn't have a meaning, what did it have? What, in the language of the new biological sciences, was its function? Through psychoanalysis, to the relief of many and to the consternation of many more, Freud was able to say two remarkable, and timely, things; suffering gave pleasure, and it was suffused with surprising (secular) news about ourselves. He described the extraordinary cultural practice called masochism as, implicitly, our best trick for survival; a way of making our inordinate suffering our profoundest pleasure, and our profoundest sexual pleasure. He described our sexuality as something we suffered; and so the meaning of our suffering was sexual. Understanding one's suffering was in the service of a more satisfying hedonism. And could itself be satisfying.

But at this period when Freud's writing and clinical practice begin to take off—when the more daunting and exhilarating Freud starts to appear—we need to pause. We need, perhaps, to bare in mind once again, as we begin to see Freud's artful science find its force and range, Freud's own reservations about biography. And here the poet Geoffrey Hill's salutary strictures about poetry and biography are useful, not least because they illuminate the subtlety of Freud's wariness. "The poets one trusts most," Hill writes, "are those who seem to suggest that art is the totality of our life and simultaneously admit that art has no connection with life."[5] This "paradox," as Hill calls it, allows us biographical speculation, and allows us not to believe a word of it. It allows us to give the always conjectural, always highly selective context of the work; and to be skeptical if not ironic about how this supposed context works in the work. Freud believed that it was impossible for art, or for anything else, to have no connection with the life of the artist. But he also believed that no one could speak, or write, on anyone else's behalf with real conviction. Psychoanalysis—though this has been easy to forget amid the clamor of Freud's perennial discrediting—was originally about people being freed to speak for themselves. The biographer—like the more conventional medical doctor with his patient—is all too often feeding his subject lines.

So we need, however sketchily, however merely factually— as is always the way with biography which must always exclude infinitely more than it can ever include: and is always sketchy, and dependent on the reassurance of facts—some sense of the so-called context, the medium in which Freud was writing his remarkable books. We need to fill in whatever might seem pertinent and useful. And especially at the point when Freud was finally becoming a man worthy of a biography; or as he suggested in his ambitious youth, when he was becoming the man who would be pursued by his biographers. Because, as the young Freud warned us, we need to acknowledge some, albeit conjectural, Freudian ground rules for the emerging biography of the man who, as we have seen, was intelligently wary of the artful ruses of biography. Who believed biographies were written, unavoidably, according to (and about) the desire of the biographer and were therefore perniciously misleading fictions. Really, from Freud's point of view, biographies were no more and no less than part of the dream-day—Freud's term for the day before the dream that supplies the material for the dream—of the reader. So certain temptations, he intimates, need to be minimized, certain conventions avoided, if we are to take seriously (or even experiment with) Freud's misgivings about biography. Or rather, if we are simply to bear them in mind. Were we to fully abide by them, of course, there would be no biography. It would be worth wondering, as Freud clearly invites us to, what kind of loss that would be?

What we don't need, then, in writing that impossible thing, a Freudian life of the young Freud, is the always fanciful (i.e., wishful), novelettish setting of scenes, and thumbnail sketches of characters, with their suppositions about what people were thinking and feeling and doing, that biography has tradition-ally traded in (like hysterical symptoms these scenes are always theatrical in their desire to move the reader, in their desire, like the hysteric, to be somehow vivid and memorable). Nor do we need to be too impressed by the plausibility of chronology, though chronology is required as an essential ingredient of any alternative narratives. The unconscious as described by Freud works with other chronologies, other pictures of cause and ef-fect, not simply the linear ones. And we certainly don't need, in the case of writers' lives, too much plot summary—or theory-summary as it might be called in Freud's case—which can only be, in Freud's terms, an obsessional symptom; something bor-ingly dutiful that Freud would be duly suspicious of (it wouldn't be the heresy of paraphrase that Freud would be alert to, but the futile violence of paraphrase). The reader needs to know what writing there was, and to be given some sense of what it might have been about, and whether—as in a psychoanalytic session—it can, aptly and occasionally, be fitted into a story of the life; useful, of course, only to the reader (if the reader wants to read the books, he needs to read the books themselves; what the biographer can offer, as that absurd figure, the ambassador for the reader's dream-day, are his idea of intriguing, evocative clues to the work). We don't, in short, need too convinced and convincing an account of what the subject thought he was doing at any given moment, and why he thought he was doing it. This, for Freud, would be faux psychoanalysis. Freud revealed to us that when it comes to motive no one can speak for anyone else. And that more often than not people resist speaking on their own behalf. Motives can only be discovered and made up in the conversation that is psychoanalysis. Freud's own biographical studies, we should remember, were short on fact, thin on chronology; fictions of very few characters, and a certain amount of rudimentary psychoanalytic speculation, often of relatively oblique details in his subjects' life. And they are all short.

There are, nevertheless, the facts—the selected facts—even of Freud's life; the requisite lists of political and personal events, of family matters, of Freud's professional achievements; all of which Freud mentioned in his correspondence during these years, none of which he is particularly excited by compared with the writing he is doing. So, for example, even though it is hardly incidental, at least in retrospect, and though Freud makes little of it, after a good twenty years of significant antisemitic propaganda in Austria—in 1889 Jews were excluded from university fraternities; in 1896 the Anti-Semitic League was formed to protect the jobs of Aryan artisans, and so on—the virulently antisemitic Christian Socialist Karl Lueger was elected mayor of Vienna in 1897. Since 1873, when Freud was sixteen, with the crash of the Vienna stock market and the inevitable antiliberal and antisemitic backlash, Freud had effectively grown up in a chronic economic recession. The election of Lueger was the ultimate confirmation of what turned out to be an irreversible trend in Viennese political life. Freud could not, of course, have been oblivious to this but he is determinedly, like many of his

Jewish contemporaries, unimpressed by it; though he is preoccupied in his professional life by the ways people repress the bad news about themselves. And, of course, Freud's family life continues, described fleetingly in his correspondence; and described very much as a world of its own, relatively unimpinged upon by the surrounding culture and ethos. In 1896, for example, Freud attended the wedding of his favourite sister, Rosa; his younger sister Pauline married and her husband died in 1900; and in the same year his half-brother Emanuel visited from England with his son Sam. But we know virtually nothing about what Freud himself made of these events. These are not the things, unsurprisingly, that Freud writes much about. The family is a taken for granted world, though Freud in his professional life was studying and treating the casualties of this taken for granted world of (often) Jewish fin de siècle Viennese bourgeois families.

Freud had often written to Fliess about the possibility of their meeting in Rome, but Freud seemed unable, somehow, to manage it. "My longing for Rome is, by the way, deeply neurotic," he wrote to Fliess in December 1897, "It is connected with my high-school hero-worship of the Semitic Hannibal, and this year, in fact, I didn't reach Rome any more than he did from Lake Trasimeno."[6] In 1901, though, Freud finally reached Rome with his brother Alexander. He described it in a letter as "a high point in my life,"[7] and his biographers have concurred, a little too complicit, perhaps, with Freud's boyhood admiration of Hannibal. Ernest Jones refers to Freud having "conquered those resistances and triumphantly entered Rome"; Gay writes of Freud's "conquest of Rome";[8] and Breger writes rather more circumspectly of what he calls Freud's "Rome neurosis" as stemming from his "identification with powerful military figures," and of Rome being associated for Freud "with one of his principal means with which he consoled himself during his childhood years of poverty and deprivation: his escape into fantasies of the ancient world."⁹ If Freud's most important invention was the idea of "dream-work," his most important principle of scientific explanation was the idea of overdetermination: that nothing psychically ever has only one cause. So, for example, though it is not surprising in psychoanalytic biographies of Freud that mastery (Jones and Gay) and self-cure for losses (Breger) would all be equally plausible contenders for understanding this high point in Freud's life—and, indeed, many other significant moments in Freud's life—neither alone can be sufficient. In his own accounts Freud never suggests a cause, he only suggests, tentatively, what could be contributory factors. Freud is always, in fact, more subtle and sceptical about the whole notion of causality than his critics assume. "Hannibal and Rome," he wrote in *Interpreting Dreams*, "symbolised the conflict between the tenacity of Jewry and the organisation of the Catholic church."¹⁰ All we can legitimately add, amidst all the possible biographical speculation, is that neither Freud nor Hannibal did conquer Rome (Freud merely went there as a tourist). And that Freud clearly valued tenacity over organization, drive over system; indeed, that he saw them as often opposed to each other. Catholicism, we should again note, was always, for Freud, the enemy. It represented what Freud despised and feared about religion.

But perhaps Freud's most important achievement in these years was not finally going to Rome, but rather the institutional achievement of finally being made a professor in the university in 1902. He needed the influence, though, of two of his more aristocratic patients; one of them, a baroness Ferstel, had to bribe the minister of education with a painting to secure the appointment (clearly, the first psychoanalyst allowed himself to use and be used by his patients; or rather, Freud allowed his patients to give him more than money). "The way to improvement," Freud wrote to one of the patients who helped him, "should not be barred to a lost soul. . . . Up to now I have heard that my activities only annoy people, and this I find quite understandable and as a first reaction just as it should be."[11] "Lost souls" were, of course, Jews, and those Christian souls lost, perhaps temporarily, to the faith, were those most in need of "improvement." The steely Freud, who is now developing a psychological account of what he calls "resistance," prides himself on the fact that he annoys people as an acknowledgment of the value of what he is doing. As a professor Freud could lecture to a wider, more curious audience; and this would play a significant part in making his new psychoanalytic ideas available. Inevitably, many of Freud's early followers had either read him or attended his lectures. He needed the prestige—the symbolic capital—of professional institutional legitimation for this to happen.

But despite these more or less significant events—that it would be misleading to call merely "background" in the work of the "great man"—we should include in an account of these extraordinary years of writing, in the way Freud taught us to, an apparently marginal detail in his work. One from his contemporary writings on dreams and jokes; both, as Freud was beginning to realize, subversive artifacts, like neurotic symptoms; ways of speaking about, of smuggling into circulation, forbidden desires. The mind, as Freud would remark in a telling analogy in *Interpreting Dreams*, was like a "political writer who has disagreeable truths to tell those in authority."[12] We should note—given that censorship condemns the explicit—that for Freud now the mind is a writer, a political one; and the individual is a state in which vigilant and punitively repressive authorities are in continual surveillance. The modern individual's "disagreeable truths" are, in Freud's view, about sexuality, but sexuality, for him, is about what people want to do together. A language for the pleasures that sustain sociability. This marginal detail, no more than ten lines of Freud's writing in this prolific period of work are about a professional Jewish man—apparently well-assimilated to his chosen culture—accused, falsely, as it happened, of treacherous writing. A man betrayed by his culture, punished, silenced and exiled; a man with passionate supporters and enemies, who divided the society that had failed him, and who was ultimately celebrated as a hero of fortitude and stoic integrity. And a man also from a country, France, that had been so important, as we have seen, in Freud's professional development.

In 1894 the Jewish French soldier Alfred Dreyfus—who had graduated ninth out of a class of eighty-two from the Ecole supérieure de guerre and was a member of the general staff of the French army—was falsely accused of treason, and spent five years in solitary confinement on Devil's Island before being finally pardoned in 1899 by the French government. Dreyfus was accused, on the basis of spurious written evidence, of spying for Germany; he was supposed to have betrayed his country from a position of influence. The case divided France, raising many ghosts of the past, not least of which was the fundamental cultural divide in French society between a patriotic, hierarchic Catholic and military elitism and the more liberal, democratic universalism that was the Enlightenment legacy of the revolution. Dreyfus's Jewishness was at the very heart of the ferocious battle between the Dreyfusards and the anti-Dreyfusards, which unleashed the virulent antisemitism that seemed to be endemic in Catholic France. "Two Frances . . . fought for the nation's soul," the historian Ruth Harris wrote, "the Dreyfusards or revisionists, defended Truth and Justice . . . the anti-Dreyfusards championed Tradition and Honour." The many Jewish Dreyfusards had to be particularly careful, Harris writes, to isolate their "Jewish rationality from the mysticism and obscurantism of the 'oriental' current."[13] The Jews who defended Dreyfus, Harris writes, used "their religious inheritance as a justification for their ethical position, but mistrusted spiritual musings and religious enthusiasm, which they thought promoted an irrational and dangerous obscurantism."[14] The Dreyfus case sent shock waves through the Jewish communities of western Europe; and made French Jews attentive once again, as Harris makes clear, to the ways they represented themselves.

In the period between the *Studies on Hysteria* and the writing of *Interpreting Dreams*—in the years, that is to say, that were the prelude and the preparation for Freud's great turn of the century writings—the Dreyfus case was of great interest in much of western Europe, and not only for the Jews. Freud, who was always so wary of psychoanalysis being considered a "Jewish science," of its seeming mystical, obscurantist ("oriental") or indeed irrational—it was supposed to be a science, a rational account of irrationality—refers to Dreyfus three times in his published writing, first in *Interpreting Dreams* and then twice in the *Joke* book, the last book written in this decisive period of his life. In a section entitled "Recent and Indifferent Material in Dreams" Freud "begins with an assertion that in every dream it is possible to find a point of contact with the experiences of the previous day." On occasion, he writes, that he begins "a dream's interpretation by looking for the event of the previous day that set it in motion." He calls the day "immediately preceding the dream," in a wonderful phrase, the "dream-day."[15] He then lists a series of his own dream images of which the final one is: "A man standing on a cliff in the middle of the sea, in the style of Bocklin. Source: Dreyfus on the Ile du Diable; I had news at the same time from my relatives in England, etc."[16] Here we have, at its most minimal, Freud identifying, at least in the manifest content of his dream, with something about the falsely accused, exiled, isolated and imprisoned Dreyfus. A cliff in the middle of the sea is not a reassuring image (perhaps an image of how Freud was feeling professionally, or in the family?). Like the Dreyfusards Freud, we might say, was in his own way, in psychoanalysis, championing truth and justice against tradition and honour (psychoanalysis strips people of a certain dignity to restore them to some kind of just truth, or another kind of truth, about themselves). Dreyfus believed that being a Jew was not a way of not being a Frenchman, much as Freud felt he could be both a Jew and an Austrian. And there is in this, perhaps, a guilty Freud who wants to believe that, like Dreyfus, he has really done nothing wrong (in inventing psychoanalysis he was just doing his job properly, he was just a Jew, like any immigrant, trying to get on in unsympathetic circumstances). In Freud's sense of things though, these are unbounded "irrational" speculations without in this case Freud, as the dreamer, being able to speak for himself (it would be "obscurantist" in Freud's terms to propose without his associations, the links in Freud's mind, say, between Bocklin, the English relatives, Dreyfus, and himself; though Freud would assume there were links). And we should notice, alerted by Freud's ear for censorship, that this reference to Dreyfus is in a section of his book entitled "Recent and Indifferent Material in Dreams." There may have been a part of Freud that would have preferred to be indifferent to the Dreyfus case.

The second reference to Dreyfus, which is in the *Joke* book, is used twice to illustrate the workings—the "play upon words," the "double-meanings"—of a certain kind of joke. As often in the joke book the joke is not very funny, and is antisemitic (as John Carey has written, "Jokes about Jews were, in a sense, the origin of Freud's book").[17] A "joking medical colleague," Freud tells us, was responsible for this joke at the time of the Dreyfus case: "This girl reminds me of Dreyfus. The army doesn't believe in her innocence."[18] In Freud's view the working of this so-called joke hangs on the word "innocence." "The word 'innocence,'" Freud writes, "on the double meaning of which the joke is constructed, has in the one context its usual meaning, with 'fault' or 'crime' as its opposite; but in the other context it has a sexual meaning, of which the opposite is 'sexual experience.'"[19]

The joke, like the dream, encodes (i.e., reveals by concealing) repressed, forbidden thoughts. And once again it is a question of what the innocent might be guilty of (and of the Jews, like sexuality itself, representing unacceptable sociability; promiscuous pleasure-and-power-seeking). It seemed clear at least to the Dreyfusards, that the only thing Dreyfus was guilty of was being a Jew; and being a Jew meant being, essentially, a saboteur of the nation-state, a person whose allegiances could not, by definition, be patriotic (and a person whose writing couldn't be trusted; who, perhaps by the same token, associated with others in unpredictable ways); and could only, by definition, be nefarious, and unfathomable to the non-Jews. We will find, perhaps unsurprisingly in Freud's work this nexus of associations of guilt, betrayal, sexuality, and Judaism; each of these having to be concealed or disguised or disowned. And each associated with dangerously unknowable affinities and allegiances (the modern question is always, who do people want to be with, and what do they want to do together?). The dream, like the joke, reveals people, from a psychoanalytic point of view, to be in hiding; consciously in hiding from the disapproving others, but unconsciously in hiding from themselves. Or rather, in hiding from the part of themselves that has wanted to fully identify with the hostile, oppressing voices in their culture (Freud was beginning to describe how our cultures live inside us more than we live in our cultures). This too Freud was beginning to discover: how thorough and destructive socialization can be, as was clear from the casualties of the particular forms of socialization that consulted him for treatment. The double meaning of innocence, Freud intimates, shows us that there is no such thing as innocence. We are always being accused, or accusing ourselves, of something. We are always guilty, which means we are perpetually self-hating.

What the Dreyfus case had made all too vivid was the precariousness of democratic liberalism; of its being haunted by its past illiberalism (by what Freud was beginning to refer to as

"the return of the repressed"). And, of course, the precariousness of the modern Jews whose very assimilation was evidence,
to their enemies, of their duplicity, their cunning. The Jews,
like any previously excluded minority, were vulnerable to a
false sense of security, out of dread and wishfulness. What
Freud's writing in these years exposed was the ways in which
modern people created a false sense of security for themselves.
Something Freud was to do himself towards the end of his life
(like the Dreyfusards he saw the Catholics as his real enemy,
rather than the Nazis). In our dreams, in our jokes, in our sexuality, in our slips—and especially in our so-called symptoms—
our real insecurities are exposed. Psychoanalysis was becoming
in Freud's writing in these years the artful science of our false
senses of security. Freud was discovering how modern people
endangered themselves by the ways in which they protected
themselves. Each of the so-called mechanisms of defense was
an unconscious form of self-blinding; ways of occluding a piece
of reality. It was this that Freud was describing in a book about
dreams, a book about mistakes, a book about sexuality, a book
about jokes, and a book about a psychoanalytic treatment. Five
books that in a real sense make up one book, albeit an often
repetitive one. If Freud had died, at the age of forty-nine, having completed these five books, psychoanalysis would have been
very different, but it would have been sufficiently complete.

The reason so much psychoanalytic writing is so dispiriting is
because it is all written by older people. Freud in his forties was a
younger man than he had ever been: less cautious and more boldly
and brashly speculative. And the writings of this period have a cor-
responding sense of exhilaration and possibility. If Freud had died
in 1906, there would have been no structural theory of the mind,
no elaborated metapsychology (the "witch metapsychology," as
Freud once referred to it), no speculation about what, if anything,
was beyond the pleasure principle, no sweeping critique of religion, and no death-drive. There would just have been a theory of

dreams, of sexuality, of jokes, of mistakes, and an intriguing clue about the practice of psychoanalysis, which would have been more than enough. And there would have been no real psychoanalytic movement over which Freud would have to preside. His work would have become what his followers made of it, unsupervised by a Master. It would always have been too early to tell what psychoanalysis really was. Indeed the subsequent history of psychoanalysis can be divided, in a sense, into those who, as it were, wished that Freud died in 1906, and those who did not.

If he had died in 1906 we would have been left just with his sophisticated account of the working of the unconscious. A fascinating and self-contradictory developmental account, in the *Three Essays*—that is both rigorously Darwinian and counter-Darwinian. A sexuality described as beginning in infancy, as essentially perverse, insatiable, unstable, excessive, endangering, ubiquitous, and therefore and thus far, in Freud's shocked and cautious view, fundamentally unintelligible; a sexuality astoundingly ingenious and inventive in its pleasure-seeking, in which cruelty is the heart of pleasure, and in which pleasure is at its most pleasurable when it is most painful; a sexuality, that is to say, which is essentially sadomasochistic and in which reproduction is both incidental and essential. But also, and more radically, an account of sexuality as sociability, as a way of living—and a way of describing—what modern people most want and fear doing together; a sexuality always normative because always subject to controlling norms, but norms modifiable not least by psychoanalysis itself. And once forms of sexuality are seen as forms of sociability it is possible to see psychoanalysis as a politics, as one modern way among many others of thinking about new styles of relating and new versions of group life. And psychoanalysis, of course, as a new discipline within medicine, was on the verge of its own group life as an international "movement," with its own terrible and salutary consequences. Psychoanalytic groups would quickly become notorious for their lack of civility and kindness. Freud initially having to write *Totem and Taboo* in 1912, and ultimately *Group Psychology and the Analysis of the Ego* in 1921, in an attempt to "work through," as he would put it, the virulent intolerance of these psychoanalytic groups.

And, if Freud had died in 1906, we would, finally, have been left with—explicitly in the *Studies on Hysteria* and the Dora case, and implicitly in Freud's other writings—the rudiments of, rather than the prescriptions for, the practice of psychoanalysis. The very few case histories would have made the potential pitfalls of psychoanalysis more than obvious: its potential for misogyny, dogmatism, and proselytizing: the analyst's temptation to speak on the patient's behalf, and to know what's best for the patient: the cultism of the analyst and patient as a couple. At this time psychoanalysis as both a theoretical and clinical practice was not yet stifled and stultified by its always anxious institutionalization. Indeed Freud's writing between 1898 and 1905, as it exposed repressed, forbidden forms of sociability—the buried-alive lives of modern people, the inextricability of their ambitions and their sexuality—created a panic that psychoanalysts, beginning with Freud, could only recover from, ironically, through repressing the discoveries of psychoanalysis itself. It would need something as strong as a putative Death Instinct—first mooted in *Beyond the Pleasure Principle* in 1920—and a daemonic repetition compulsion to counter and condemn the extravagant vital energies, the sexual energies, Freud was finding in his most disturbed patients. So much aliveness in modern individuals—and in psychoanalysis itself—required its antidote. On the one hand there was neurosis, but on the other hand there could be psychoanalysis, especially in its overinstitutionalised forms. After 1906 it became increasingly clear that psychoanalysis, ironically, was to be a profession more obsessed by enforcing its own rules of theory and practice than by wondering what rules are being used for. In the traditional Jewish way, desire for the law would trump all other desires. It was not clear initially—and not only to Freud's critics—which side of the law psychoanalysts were on; it soon would be. After Darwin human beings seemed to be the only animals whose sexuality was a problem. Freud was to describe what kind of problem it was. The young Freud had realized—though he was not keen to fully acknowledge the radical implications of this—that problems about sex were problems about the law. By redescribing sexuality you could change the norms that governed it.

In retrospect we can see Freud havering in these years as to whether people were suffering from their sexual desire or from their self-cures for their sexual desire. Whether neurotic symptoms were, as he put it, a poor "compromise" for the neurotic, between his sexual desire and his defenses against it, and better compromises were required. Or whether, as the sexual liberators among his later followers believed—Wittels and Reich being the most insistent—psychoanalysis was a freeing up of desire (a proving that the inhibition was irrelevant, as one prominent psychoanalyst would later say). Freud's emphasis on sexuality—and on sexuality as a language game—in other words, in these formative years of psychoanalysis, was as much a working out of what (modern) sexuality might be—what the word was about—as it was a defining of what sexuality essentially was; and we see Freud doing both things in his writing.

But Freud had not, of course, discovered sex, he had added something to the long cultural conversation about it. Something about sexuality as the material of sociability; sexuality as what we make our sociability out of. Sexuality as something we make, but like political writers who have to keep their eye on the authorities.

So Michel Foucault was doing no more than stating a plain truth when he wrote of the celebrants of Freud that, what they had attributed solely to the genius of Freud had already gone through a long stage of preparation; they had gotten their dates wrong as to the establishment in our society, of a general deployment of sexuality . . . they believed that Freud had, at last, through a sudden reversal, restored to sex the rightful share which it had been denied for so long; they had not seen how the good genius of Freud had placed it at one of the critical points marked out for it since the eighteenth century by the strategies of knowledge and power, how wonderfully effective he was—worthy of the greatest spiritual fathers and directors of the classical period—in giving a new impetus to the secular injunction to study sex and transform it into discourse.[20]

It would be easy (and instructive), in the light of this, to see Freud's early life as, say, simply a modern parable of the rediscovery of sex by an unusual individual in a particular culture at a particular time; akin, say, to the life of Havelock Ellis, or D. H. Lawrence, or Wilhelm Reich. But what Freud was interested in in these crucial years was not just the all-too-familiar, all-too-human imperious urgency of sex, but how the body becomes (in both senses) its languages; how culture is the translation, to use one of Freud's favoured analogies, of the body's unconscious, forbidden desire, the desire a person believes he can't afford to acknowledge. Freud was not returning sexuality to its "rightful share," but working out what that share might be.

Freud, at the turn of the century, did not have the language to see this process of ineluctable acculturation by which he was increasingly fascinated, as embedded in "strategies of knowledge and power" (this would be Foucault's contribution: and it is a useful way of reading the subsequent history of psychoanalysis). But the real scandal of Freud's work at this time—displaced, to use one of his terms, onto the idea of infantile sexuality—was his discovery of just how ingenious and disturbing modern people had become as the unconscious artists of their own lives. It was their capacities for representation—for finding ways and means for making their desires known in however disguised or self-defeating forms; as dreams, or slips, or perverse and neurotic symptoms—that had impressed Freud. What could be done with—how something is made out of—the virtually unassimilable material of sexual desire and aggression. His patients, Freud realized, were working on and at their psychic survival, but like artists not like scientists; and their material was their personal history encoded in their sexuality. They were not empiricists, or only fleetingly; they were fantasists. Their adaptations were ingeniously imaginative, however painful; but they were stuck. Their symptoms were the equivalent of writer's block, or rather, speaker's block. Indeed, Freud was becoming their new kind of good listener, and their champion; someone who could get, who could make something of, their strange ways of speaking. Someone who, like a good parent, or a good art critic, could appreciate what they were up to, what they could make, and make a case for it.

Freud coined the term "dream-work" in *Interpreting Dreams* because the dream was, in his view, something the dreamer made. Through what he called, in Chapter 6 of *Interpreting Dreams*, the four "mechanisms" of the dream-work, condensation, displacement, considerations of representability, and secondary revision—mechanisms because they were the virtually automatic unconscious skills of the dreamer as artisan—the dreamer "wove" out of the perceived materials of the day (the "dream day") what Freud called a "disguised fulfillment of a childhood wish." Through the materials of the present, recruited by the repressed desires from the distant past, the dreamer formulated what he wanted, but in disguised form to get round the censor. In our dreams, Freud proposed, we are the historians—if not the archivists—of our own desire, making something to look forward to, something to want, out of the desires of the past. Reminding ourselves of what we might want from what we once wanted.

What we can't help but do, though often unbeknownst to ourselves and to others—at least, consciously—is make our unacceptable desires known, is make them public. This, in Freud's view, is what dreams, and jokes and slips, and neurotic symptoms all do, because they are essentially similar kinds of artifacts, structured according to their function; each of them uses the mechanisms of the dream-work to transform unconscious desire into acceptable forms of knowledge and action. And these artifacts make us wonder, by the same token—as Freud would wonder later in his more sociological works like *Civilisation and Its Discontents* of 1930—what kind of societies we have created that require these kinds of suffering, this kind of art, this frustrating adaptive inventiveness. All these artifacts reveal, above all for Freud, people's unacceptable intentions; like the president of the Austrian parliament whom Freud cites in the *Psychopathology of Everyday Life*, opened a session by saying, "Gentleman: I take notice that a full quorum of members is present and herewith declare the sitting closed,"[21] Freud is always showing us how much more people are always saying—to themselves and to others—than they consciously intend. Wanting to stop things before they begin, and not knowing when to stop were, for Freud, an emblem of the modern person's predicament. Freud is not showing us merely that we are unacceptable to ourselves, but that we are more complicated than we want to be. And more wishful. And more frustrated. And more and less divided against ourselves than we may need to be.

It was unconscious "making" that Freud had become interested in in these early years; how our desires were made into wishes and our wishes were made known (it is not incidental that the *Psychopathology of Everyday Life*—Freud's most widely read work, published in eleven editions and translated into twelve languages in his lifetime—is a psychopathology of making, of making slips). Perhaps it is not surprising that Freud, in the process of making himself the psychoanalyst he was becoming, wrote his five key books about making—about the making of dreams, the making of mistakes, the making of sexual preferences, the making of jokes, and, above all given his nominal profession, the making of symptoms. And in the case of "Dora" he would also give us a glimpse of what a doctor had to do to make himself a practicing psychoanalyst, for better and for worse. Though Freud, as a scientist, claims to be discovering and describing "natural" processes—in the language of biology he is giving an account of structure according to function—he is, without saying so, in these years, describing the dreamer, the bungler, the sexual person, the joker, the neurotic, and, indeed, the psychoanalyst, as artists (sometimes slapstick, sometimes not); as people with remarkable gifts for creating elaborate and subtle, intriguing, and amusing artifacts, with proliferating meanings and uses, in the service of psychic survival. The Romantic myth of the suffering artist has been transformed, by Freud, into the story of everyone. With the publication of these five extraordinary books Freud was about to discover what people made of what he had made. Which would become, at once, the history of psychoanalysis, and the history of the second half of Freud's life. Years in which Europe would disintegrate into two cataclysmic world wars, and psychoanalysis would begin to flourish as a revolutionary new science. There were many talented eccentric people drawn to Freud and his work, waiting in the wings of what would become an international psychoanalytic movement.

After the age of fifty Freud's life, not unlike his earlier years, will be a series of meetings with remarkable men, and of fewer meetings with remarkable women (two of whom, Sabina Speilrein and Lou Andreas-Salome, would make decisive contributions to psychoanalysis). It will be a life of what became known as psychoanalytic politics, as Freud revises and refines—and occasionally turns against and betrays—his first real psychoanalytic writing of these crucial years amid the collapsing politics of central Europe. Above all, at least from Freud's own point of view, it will be a life of prolific and remarkable writing. Writing done, in a very real sense, in the aftermath, in the fallout, of the great five books he wrote at the turn of the century. And in anticipation, we might be tempted to think now, of the catastrophes to come.

Epilogue

. . . once doctrine is sighted and is held to be the
completion of insight, the doctrinal note of thinking
seems the only one possible. When doctrine totters
it seems it can fall only into the gulf of bewilder-
ment; few minds risk the fall; most seize the
remnants and swear the edifice remains, when
doctrine becomes intolerable dogma.
—R. P. Blackmur, *The Double Agent*

"WHEN WE SCRUTINISE the personalities who, by self-selection became the first generation of psychoanalysts," Freud's
daughter Anna wrote in 1968 in her Freud anniversary lecture
"Difficulties in the Path of Psychoanalysis,"

> we are left in no doubt about their characteristics. They
> were the unconventional ones, the doubters, those who were
> dissatisfied with the limitations imposed on knowledge; also

among them were the odd ones, the dreamers, and those who knew neurotic suffering from their own experience. This type of intake has altered decisively since psychoanalytic training has become institutionalised and appeals in this stricter form to a different type of personality. Moreover, self-selection has given way to the careful scrutiny of applicants, resulting in the exclusion of the mentally endangered, the eccentrics, the self-made, those with excessive flights of imagination, and favouring the acceptance of the sober, well-prepared ones, who are hard working enough to wish to better their professional efficiency.[1]

Freud himself has warned us of the dangers of nostalgia. And Anna Freud, who became a psychoanalyst herself, having been analysed by her father—one of the ultimate taboos of latter day psychoanalysis—became a key player in the institutionalization of psychoanalysis after the war. And yet what she is lamenting is a part, at least, of the history of psychoanalysis, a history that began, effectively, towards the end of the first decade of the twentieth century. As Alfred Adler, Carl Jung, Sandor Ferenczi, Otto Rank, Wilhelm Reich, Karl Abraham, Paul Federn, and Ernest Jones—the most prominent, among many others—came to meet and work with Freud during this time, national and international psychoanalytic societies sprung up, journals were published, rules for membership and clinical practice were drawn up. Though Freud's actual working practices were often far removed from his (relatively few) strictures on psychoanalytic technique, he had published guidelines on psychoanalytic practice; though interestingly they were never as extensive, it should be said, as his colleagues, particularly Ferenczi and Jones, had wished (there can be no technique for improvisation, only techniques that make improvisation possible). By the time Freud died in 1939 there was a thriving new profession when thirty years previously there had been no such profession, and psychoanalysis had been, until around 1906, a subspecialty within the contemporary medicine of the time. And yet its rigorous institutionalisation would come at some cost. As the anthropologist Mary Douglas pointed out—and it is of a piece with Anna Freud's plea—"Any institution that is going to keep its shape needs to control the memory of its members." It was soon forgotten that psychoanalysis was a profession for dreamers.[2]

What Anna Freud fails to mention is that her father in his youth had himself, in his own respectable way, been one of "those who were dissatisfied with the limitations imposed on knowledge . . . the odd ones, the dreamers, and those who knew neurotic suffering from their own experience." He was, if not obviously one of the "mentally endangered, the eccentrics," he was one of the "self-made," a person with "excessive flights of imagination" even if he preferred to think of them as more pronounced in other people than in himself. It would always be people with these supposedly excessive flights of imagination that he was drawn to, as both patients and colleagues. The bourgeois caricature of the sober Freud—the "Doctor," "the Master" with the beady eye—we need to remember, is largely the product of the iconography of his middle and late years.

And we need to remember that the older Freud, presumably with retrospective misgivings about his own early training, was always a champion, against much opposition within the profession he had invented, of what was called, in an unfortunate phrase "lay analysis," the training of nonmedical psychoanalysts. Freud, in other words, did not believe that a training in medicine, or even in the sciences, was a prerequisite for the work of a psychoanalyst. And he believed this to the end of his life: "I have never repudiated these views," he wrote in 1938, "and I insist upon them even more intensely than before."[3] Though he always held to the value of science as self-correcting and consensually empirical, his new science of psychoanalysis had also shown him the limits of scientific method. Science abstracted and overgeneralized the singularity, the profounder eccentricity of human character that psychoanalysis revealed. Indeed in its description of character psychoanalysis often seemed to begin where science left off—that is, with the irreducible uniqueness of individual temperament and history. Psychoanalytic case histories sounded like short stories, in Freud's formulation, because they were short stories; they were strikingly unlike the medical writing of the times. When Freud eventually referred to the instincts, the fundamental building blocks of Darwinian biology, as his "mythology"; when he proposed the instinctual dualism of life as a battle between the life instinct and the death instinct in *Beyond the Pleasure Principle* (1920), and gave these instincts the mythological names of Eros and Thanatos, he was making scientific method compatible with mythmaking. We need to see Freud's abiding fascination with the making and consuming of fictions beginning in his youth, as he taught us to do in his own idiosyncratic way. His medical training, he thought of, ironically, as part of his misspent youth. An eccentric and, as it turned out, a remarkable dreamer, he had by his own account temporarily lost his way by studying medicine.

It is worth noting that the whole subject of lay analysis made Freud uncharacteristically autobiographical. In his *Postscript to the Question of Lay Analysis* (1926), at the age of seventy and so free of the constraints of his youth, he wrote:

> After forty years of medical activity, my self-knowledge tells me that I have never really been a doctor in the proper sense. I became a doctor through being compelled to deviate from my original purpose; and the triumph of my life lies in my having, after a long and roundabout journey, found my way back to my earliest path. . . . In my youth I felt an overpowering need to understand something of the riddles of the world in which we live, and perhaps even to contribute some-

thing to their solution. The most hopeful means of achiev-
ing this end seemed to be to enroll myself in the medical
faculty. . . . I scarcely think, however, that my lack of a genuine medical temperament has done much damage to my
patients.[4]

It seemed to be but it was not. Freud intimates, without
quite saying so, that lacking "a genuine medical temperament"
might have done more than merely not harmed his patients.
"Indeed," Freud goes on, "the words, 'secular pastoral worker'
might well serve as a general formula for describing the function which the analyst, whether he is a doctor or a layman, has
to perform in his relation to the public."[5] In the really very
difficult task of finding analogies for the practice of psychoanalysis Freud always needed it to be not only a rational account
of the irrational, but also a reputable account of the disreputable.
More ambitious than Oedipus, the young Freud had wanted to
understand the riddles of the world; it was a quest for knowledge, as we saw at the beginning, that Freud was inspired by,
but on a grand scale. Medicine turned out to be a wrong turning, a deviation. Through psychoanalysis he found a different
kind of riddle—a riddle from ancient myth—and different solutions; his preferred phrase for the psychoanalyst—not doctor
but "secular pastoral worker"—sounds like a new version of a
very much older, more traditional role. But psychoanalysis,
Freud is clear is, above all, neither a medical treatment, nor a
conversion experience:

> We do not seek to bring [the patient] relief by receiving him
> into the catholic, protestant or socialist community. We seek
> rather to enrich him from his own internal resources, by put-
> ting at the disposal of his ego those energies which, owing to
> repression, are inaccessibly confined in his unconscious, as
> well as those which his ego is obliged to squander in the fruit-
> less task of maintaining these repressions. Such activity as
> this is pastoral work in the best sense of the words.[6]

Freud, who conspicuously doesn't mention Judaism (or Zionism) certainly uses the idea of pastoral work in the most ironic of senses; the pastoral work of psychoanalysis is about liberating energies, allowing the individual access to his inner resources, irrespective, at least in the first instance, of their moral value. Psychoanalysis, then, is neither a science in the usual sense, nor a religion in the traditional sense; he wants it to be an unusual science, and somehow akin to a secular religion. Freud writes that he wants "to feel assured that the therapy will not destroy the science,"[7] knowing that it might, but wanting to have this both ways. Psychoanalysis had helped Freud understand his ambivalence about science (ambivalence was Freud's self-cure for fanaticism). He wanted, and found through psychoanalysis, freedom from some of the limitations imposed upon knowledge by both science and religion.

Psychoanalysis then, Freud's life's work—that in one sense was finished and in another sense just beginning in 1906—invites us to imagine, in his daughter's words, what "those who were [then] dissatisfied with the limitations imposed on knowledge," might want knowledge to be and to do for them; to imagine, that is to say, what satisfactions these dissatisfactions might lead to. Anna Freud was not a bohemian herself, nor was she given to glamourising the rebellious, but her message was clear in that fateful year 1968—psychoanalysis was originally a science for outsiders.

But we need to remember, by way of conclusion, that despite Freud's equivocations about science and his essential and constitutive uncertainty about what kind of thing psychoanalysis was, Freud—who had no truck with the supernatural—believed in telepathy much to the dismay of his first official biographer and disciple, the Welsh psychoanalyst Ernest Jones. "There is no doubt," Jones wrote in his chapter in his official biography of Freud on occultism, that [telepathy] is by far the most "respectable" element in the field of occultism, and therefore the one that has gained the widest acceptance. In Freud's opinion it probably represented the kernel of truth in that field, one which the myth-making tendencies of mankind had enveloped in a cocoon of phantastic beliefs. The idea of a "kernel of truth" specially fascinated Freud and cooperated with more personal motives in his unconscious to incline him towards accepting a belief in telepathy. He had more than once had the experience of discovering such a kernel in the complicated beliefs of mankind, beliefs often contemptuously dismissed as superstition; that dreams really had a meaning was the most important element. So he felt intuitively that telepathy might be the kernel of truth in this obscure field.[8]

The question to be asked of every biographer is, what does he want to guarantee that his subject is not? Freud's biographers have wanted to assure their readers that Freud is not a charlatan; a spurious version of a real thing; Freud as the arch unmasker that needs to be unmasked himself (of course the Jews of Freud's generation, like all second generation immigrants, were struggling to be, or to seem to be, the real thing, as defined by their host cultures). Jones is clearly bending over backwards to defend Freud's credulity and his credibility here, as if he doesn't want us to get the wrong idea (that Freud was also a crank); as if, like all biographers, as I say, there are things he is trying to stop us thinking about his subject (only Freud's noble passion for truth could have made him take this stuff seriously). Though he noticeably tells us nothing in this passage of what Freud's unconscious personal motives might be, thus casting some suspicion, Jones wants to reassure us with the "kernel of truth" idea. As long as Truth is being pursued, as long as the quest for true knowledge, however misguided, is in play, we can go on taking Freud seriously (the question about psychoanalysts has always been whether or in what way to take

them seriously). What, we might wonder, has the biographer—
especially the biographer of a psychoanalyst, and of *the* psychoanalyst—got to be defensive about? Why shouldn't, why wouldn't
the founder of psychoanalysis be interested in telepathy? And
what, say, from a psychoanalytic point of view, might this tell us
about his character? When Jones began to question Freud about
this Freud replied in a letter of 7 March 1926:

> If someone should reproach you with my Fall into Sin, you
> are free to reply that my adherence to telepathy is my pri-
> vate affair like my Jewishness, my passion for smoking, and
> other things, and the theme of telepathy—inessential for
> psychoanalysis.[9]

It is a strikingly subtle and complicated sentence. Freud immediately suggests that it is Jones's amour propre that is at stake
not his own ("if someone should reproach you. . ."); Jones is
dearly worried what it might say about him to be the follower
(Jones's word) of a man interested in telepathy. It is, Freud as-
serts his "private affair"—though known to many of his colleagues—and thereby "inessential" for psychoanalysis, Freud thus
disidentifying himself from psychoanalysis, and saying that some
things are private, i.e., exempt even from psychoanalysis (he
was showing us that you can love psychoanalysis and love other
things more). He has a private life that is not relevant to psychoanalysis—there is more to him than psychoanalysis could
or should encompass—and psychoanalysis (and psychoanalysts) must leave some things alone. They mustn't attempt to
colonise people's privacy. And then there is Freud's list of his
private affairs. Sexuality, perhaps unsurprisingly, is not mentioned; and the two other things mentioned—and linked to telepathy—could not be more public, Jewishness and smoking.

The psychoanalyst can't help but ask why these three things,
and what links them? They are all, perhaps, intimate unspoken
pleasures; forms of community or communion smoking, say, as

self-communing, and so on, a private, mostly unconscious, sociability. All of them, of course, are disapproved of by the authorities: it is not good to believe in them. And then, or rather, right at the beginning of the sentence, there is Freud comparing his "adherence to telepathy" (different from the "theme of telepathy") to the Fall into Sin; that is, as a desire for forbidden knowledge. As if telepathy, like smoking and, indeed, Jewishness, give Freud access to a forbidden, fateful knowledge that he shouldn't want, but can't resist. And enjoys despite their consequences. And in the original story this knowledge was provided by a woman.

Judaism, the genesis myth tells us, was the consequence of the Fall, but in this letter telepathy is Freud's original sin; his descriptions of the unofficial ways in which people communicate with themselves and each other, a sin that Freud equates with the profoundest pleasure, as he would with all sins. People are reading each other's minds all the time whether they realize it or not; Freud's psychoanalysis just follows on from there. That is what Freud wants to keep private; this acknowledgement is his private pleasure. What people did without realizing, without noticing what they were doing; the secular redescription of transgression, and the link between transgression and knowledge; people's ineluctable sociability, despite their determined attempts to isolate themselves; the relentless inventiveness of conscious and unconscious communication between people. These, after all, were the themes of his psychoanalysis. The unofficial, the unspoken, the disapproved of, the disreputable, all as somehow essential for a kind of sociability Freud had intimations of, and that psychoanalysis would begin by describing. But the psychoanalysis that the young Freud invented—emblematically represented here as telepathy, Jewishness, and cigars—was, like its younger founder, something of uncertain status. Something it was difficult to know what to make of. Something for those eccentrics and dreamers who don't know what to make of themselves.

S.E. citations refer to *The Complete Psychological Works of Sigmund Freud* (Standard Edition), 24 vols. (New York: W.W. Norton, 1976). All other quotations from Freud, including titles, are from the New Penguin Freud Translations.

1. Freud's Impossible Life

1. S.E. XVI, 300.
2. S.E. II, 160.
3. S.E. VII, 243.
4. S.E. VII, 149.
5. S.E. XXI, 231.
6. S.E. XX, 8.
7. S.E. XVIII, 59.
8. Sigmund Freud, *The Sigmund Freud-Ludwig Binswanger Correspondence, 1908–1938,* ed. Gerhard Fichtner, trans. Arnold J. Pomerans and with introduction, editorial notes, and additional letters translated by Tom Roberts (London: Open Gate Press, 2003).

9. Ernst Freud, ed., *Letters of Sigmund Freud* (London: Hogarth Press, 1961), 127 (31.5.1936).

10. S.E. XI, 130.

11. Freud, *Letters*, 152.

12. Peter Gay, *Freud: A Life for Our Time* (New York: Anchor, 1989), 504.

13. Ibid., 505.

2. Freud from the Beginning

1. S.E. XIII, 259.

2. Ibid., 268.

3. Quoted in Louis Breger, *Freud: Darkness in the Midst of Vision* (New York: Wiley, 2001), 361.

4. Esther Benbassa, *Suffering as Identity: The Jewish Paradigm*, trans. G. M. Goshgarian (New York: Verso, 2010), 40.

5. Ibid.

6. David Vital, *A People Apart: The Jews in Europe, 1789–1939* (Oxford: Oxford University Press, 1999), 298.

7. Adam Sutcliffe, *Judaism and Enlightenment* (Cambridge: Cambridge University Press, 2003), 261.

8. Peter Gay, *Freud: A Life for Our Time* (New York: Anchor, 1989), 6.

9. Mike Rapport, *1848 Year of Revolution* (London, 2008), 174.

10. See S.E. XXI, 60.

11. Ibid., 33.

12. Sigmund Freud, *The Uncanny*, ed. Hugh Haughton (London: Penguin, 2003), 21.

13. Hendrik Marinus Ruitenbeek, *Freud as We Knew Him* (Detroit: Wayne State University Press, 1973), 141.

14. Ibid., 141–42.

15. S.E. XXII, 123.

16. Gay, *Freud*, 7.

17. Quoted in Ernest Jones, *The Life and Work of Sigmund Freud* (New York: Basic, 1953), 1:45.

18. S.E. IV, 197.

19. S.E. XXI, 145.

20. Malcolm Bowie, *Psychoanalysis and the Future of Theory* (Oxford: Blackwell, 1993), 11.

21. Ruitenbeck, *Freud as We Knew Him*, 142.

22. S.E. XX, 8.

23. Quoted in Gay, *Freud*, 601.

24. Quoted in Armstrong, *A Compulsion for Antiquity* (Ithaca, NY: Cornell University Press, 2005), 25.

25. S.E. XX, 8.

26. S.E. XIII, 241.

27. Armstrong, *Compulsion*, 29.

28. Quoted in Breger, *Freud*, 36.

29. Quoted in Gay, *Freud*, 24.

30. Ibid.

31. Isidor Sadger, *Recollecting Freud*, ed., trans., and introduction by Alan Dundes (Madison, WI: University of Wisconsin Press, 2005), 19.

32. S.E. XX, 9.

33. Ibid.

34. Barry Richards, *The Jewish World of Sigmund Freud: Essays on Cultural Roots and the Problem of Religious Identity* (Jefferson, NC: McFarland, 2010), 22.

35. Leora Faye Batnitzky, *How Judaism Became a Religion: An Introduction to Modern Jewish Thought* (Princeton: Princeton University Press, 2011), 4.

36. Jacques Rancière, *The Ignorant Schoolmaster: Five Lessons in Intellectual Emancipation*, trans. Kristin Ross (Stanford, CA: Stanford University Press, 1991), 35.

37. Sadger, *Recollecting Freud*, 19.

38. S.E. XVIII, 129, 135.

39. S.E. XXI, 64–65.

40. Katja Behling, *Martha Freud: A Biography* (Cambridge: Polity Press, 2005), 13.

41. Ibid., 14.

42. Ibid., 19.

43. Ibid., 27.

44. Ibid., 28.

45. Ibid., 31.

46. Sigmund Freud, *An Autobiographical Study* (New York: Norton, 1989 [reissue]), 9.

47. Richards, *Jewish World*, 51.

48. Ibid.

49. Ibid.

50. S.E. XIII, 181–82.

51. S.E. XV, 21.

52. Jonathan Lear, *Freud* (London: Routledge, 2005), 7.

53. Freud, *Autobiographical Study*, 10.

54. S.E. XX, 10.

55. S.E. XI, 135.

3. Freud Goes to Paris

1. Peter Gay, *Freud: A Life for Our Time* (New York: Anchor, 1989), 48.

2. Ibid.

3. Louis Breger, *Freud: Darkness in the Midst of Vision* (New York: Wiley, 2001), 75.

4. Ibid.

5. Richard Poirier, *The Performing Self: Compositions and De-compositions in the Languages of Contemporary Life* (New Brunswick, NJ: Rutgers University Press, 1992), xxii.

6. Ibid., 87.

7. Breger, *Freud*, 76.

8. Andrew Scull, *Hysteria: The Disturbing History* (Oxford: Oxford University Press, 2009), 107.

9. Ibid., 105.

10. S.E. III, 16.

11. Scull, *Hysteria*, 110.

12. Ernest Jones, *The Life and Work of Sigmund Freud* (New York: Basic, 1953–57), 1:76.

13. S.E. XX, 12.

14. S.E. XIV, 14.

15. Ibid.

16. Ibid.

17. Ibid.

18. Ibid., 22.

19. Gay, *Freud*, 50.

20. Breger, *Freud*, 85.

21. S.E. III, 17.

22. Frank J. Sulloway, *Freud, Biologist of the Mind: Beyond the Psychoanalytic Legend* (Cambridge: Harvard University Press, 1992), 30.

23. Quoted in Breger, *Freud*, 79.

24. Ibid., 80.

25. Ibid., 75.

26. Ibid., 77.

27. Ernst L. Freud, ed., *Letters of Sigmund Freud* (New York: Basic, 1960), 188.

28. Breger, *Freud*, 77.

29. Sulloway, *Freud*, 51.

30. Jones, *Life and Work*, 1:223.

31. Freud, *Letters*, 413.

32. S.E. XX, 19.

33. S.E. III, 268–71.

34. Alasdair MacIntyre, *Marcuse* (London: Fontana, 1970), 41.

35. S.E. II, 160.

36. George Makari, *Revolution in Mind: The Creation of Psychoanalysis* (New York: Harper 2008), 39.

37. Breger, *Freud*, 105.

38. S.E. XIX, 289.

4. Freud Begins to Dream

1. Ernest Jones, *The Life and Work of Sigmund Freud* (New York: Basic, 1953–57), 2:158–59.

2. Louis Breger, *Freud: Darkness in the Midst of Vision* (New York: Wiley, 2001), 129.

3. Mark Edmundson, *Towards Reading Freud: Self-Creation in Milton, Wordsworth, Emerson, and Sigmund Freud* (Princeton: Princeton University Press, 1990), ix.

4. S.E. XX, 18.

5. Peter Gay, *Freud: A Life for Our Time* (New York: Anchor, 1989), 130.

6. Breger, *Freud*, 126.

7. Ibid., 127.

8. Ibid.

9. Ibid., 135.

10. Ibid.

11. Gay, *Freud*, 61.

12. Ibid., 60.

13. Breger, *Freud*, 151.

14. Masud Khan, *The Privacy of the Self* (London: Hogarth, 1974), 107.

15. Breger, *Freud*, 30.

16. Gay, *Freud*, 56–57.

17. Ibid., 62.

18. Breger, *Freud*, 136–37.

19. Ibid., 128.

20. Ibid., 129.

21. Ibid.

22. Ibid.

23. Ibid., 130.

24. Gay, *Freud*, 61.

25. Breger, *Freud*, 143.

26. *The Origins of Psychoanalysis* (London: Hogarth, 1954), 25.

27. Ibid., 26.

28. Ibid., 396.

29. Quoted in Adam Phillips, *On Balance* (New York: Farrar, Straus and Giroux, 2010), 133–34.

5. Psychoanalysis Comes Out

1. Louis Breger, *Freud: Darkness in the Midst of Vision* (New York: Wiley, 2001), 164.

2. George Makari, *Revolution in Mind: The Creation of Psychoanalysis* (New York: Harper, 2008), 133.

3. S.E. VII, 116.

4. Breger, *Freud*, 177.

5. *Essays in Criticism* LXIII (January 2013): 1.

6. Breger, *Freud*, 160.

7. Ibid.

8. Ibid.

9. Ibid., 161.

10. Ibid., 160.

11. Ernst L. Freud, ed., *Letters of Sigmund Freud* (New York: Basic, 1960), 253.

12. Makari, *Revolution*, 79.

13. Ruth Harris, *The Man on Devil's Island: Alfred Dreyfus and the Affair That Divided France* (London: Penguin, 2011), 3, 191.

14. Ibid., 373.

15. S.E. IV, 165–66.

16. Ibid.

17. Sigmund Freud, *The Joke and Its Relation to the Unconscious*, with introduction by John Cary (London: Penguin, 2003), xxv.

18. S.E. VIII, 40.

19. Ibid.

20. Michel Foucault, *The History of Sexuality: The Will to Knowledge* (London: Penguin, 1998), 1:159.

21. S.E. VI, 59.

Epilogue

1. Anna Freud, *Problems of Psychoanalytic Technique and Therapy* (London, Hogarth Press, 1972), 133.

2. Mary Douglas, *How Institutions Think* (Syracuse, 1982), 112.

3. S.E. XX, 181.

4. S.E. XX, 253–54.

5. Ibid., 255–56.

6. Ibid., 256.

7. Ibid., 254.

8. Ernest Jones, *The Life and Work of Sigmund Freud* (New York: Basic, 1953–57), 3:38.

9. Peter Gay, *Freud: A Life for Our Time* (New York: Anchor, 1989), 445.

ACKNOWLEDGMENTS

THIS BOOK IS BASED ON the Clark Lectures that I was invited to give at Trinity College, Cambridge, in the spring of 2014. I am very grateful to the master and fellows of the college for their invitation to give these particular lectures, and for their hospitality; and, indeed to the audiences for their attentive interest. Different versions of some of this book were given as lectures at the University of York where, as usual, colleagues and students contributed a great deal to the final form of this book. What became the first chapter of this book was also given, again in slightly different form, as a lecture at Wolfson College, Oxford; Hermione Lee's invitation to give this lecture came at a good time, and helped me think rather more about biography.

A conversation with Hugh Haughton freed me to finish this book, and after what is now nearly forty years of conversation probably made it possible for me to write it in the first place. Without our friendship I would not have been able to imagine myself as I do. Michael Neve, John Forrester, Lisa Appignanesi, Tom Weaver, Matt Bevis, Kit Fann, David Russell, Geoffrey Weaver, Kate Weaver, John Gray, Simon Prosser, Mark Phillips, Chris Oakley, Paul Holdengraber, Robert Mc-Rum, Simon Winder, Barbara Taylor, and Norma Clark have all made various remarks along the way that have helped me think about the book. I have been extremely fortunate to have Ileene Smith as my editor at Yale. I'm not sure I could have written this book without the sense I have had that she got what I was wanting to do. Judith Clark has done far more for this particular book than she may realise.

INDEX

Jewish Lives is a major series of interpretive biography designed to illuminate the imprint of Jewish figures upon literature, religion, philosophy, politics, cultural and economic life, and the arts and sciences. Subjects are paired with authors to elicit lively, deeply informed books that explore the range and depth of Jewish experience from antiquity through the present.

Jewish Lives is a partnership of Yale University Press and the Leon D. Black Foundation.

Ileene Smith is editorial director. Anita Shapira and Steven J. Zipperstein are series editors.